13

VERY AMAZING
ANIMALS
and How God Used Them

DAVID **C** COOK™

transforming lives together

13 VERY AMAZING ANIMALS AND HOW GOD USED THEM
Published by David C Cook
4050 Lee Vance Drive
Colorado Springs, CO 80918 U.S.A.

David C Cook U.K., Kingsway Communications
Eastbourne, East Sussex BN23 6NT, England

The graphic circle C logo is a registered trademark of David C Cook.

All Scripture quotations are taken from the Holy Bible, New Living Translation,
copyright © 1996, 2007 by Tyndale House Foundation. Used by permission of
Tyndale House Publishers, Inc., Carol Stream, Illinois 60188. All rights reserved.

LCCN 2017952572
ISBN 978-1-4347-1254-7
eISBN 978-0-8307-7295-7

© 2018 David C Cook

The Team: Lindsay Black, Amy Konyndyk, Rachael Stevenson,
Lynn Pratt, Abby DeBenedittis, Susan Murdock
Cover Design/Illustration: Dennis Jones

Printed in the United States of America

1 2 3 4 5 6 7 8 9 10

011518

"And then I heard every creature in heaven and on earth and under the earth and in the sea. They sang: 'Blessing and honor and glory and power belong to the one sitting on the throne and to the Lamb forever and ever.'"

Revelation 5:13

Contents

How to Use These
Sessions

About These Sessions

First, thanks. Thanks for caring about children and for helping them explore how God has used animals to make himself and his purposes known. Because God *has* done some remarkable things through his furry, fuzzy, and funny creations. A talking donkey? A fish carrying around a tax payment in its mouth? A rooster reminder that brought a grown man to his knees?

You'll help your kids explore all those events and experience powerful transformation as they link Bible truths they need with the animals they love. It's learning and delight—all rolled into one fun session.

So get ready to have some fun! You'll help change young lives and turn tender hearts toward Jesus. Soak in the laughter and see kids transformed.

What could be more fun than that?

Welcome to Easy

These sessions for elementary kids are carefully designed to make your life easy. They're light on supplies, quick to prepare, and long on fun. You'll find most supplies in the church's supply closet or kitchen or at home in your garage, pantry, or junk drawer—no need to spend time ordering materials online.

Because these sessions are created so beginning teachers or mature teenagers can lead them confidently, you won't need highly trained teachers. And the variety of options in each session will snag—and hold—the attention of first-grade through sixth-grade children, including the boys!

Best of all, you'll see kids grow in their faith as they open their hearts to what God shares with them through these 13 sessions.

Welcome to **Simple Learning**

Preparation is easy too. Each session, you'll focus on one key Bible truth, which children will explore and apply. You'll drive that point home through Bible exploration, fun discussions, giggle-worthy games, and "Oh, wow!" activities that engage kids in multiple ways through multiple learning styles.

Welcome to **Deep Bible Discovery**

Each session, your children actually *experience* a Bible truth. They'll discover it, ponder it, talk about it, pray about it, and apply what they learn. If that's what you're looking for—for your children to *do* God's Word instead of just hear it—you're in exactly the right place. And here's a tip: supersize the learning by using a kid-friendly version of the Bible to make sure the stories are understood by children.

Welcome to **Flexibility**

We get it: sometimes you have to punt. A sermon goes long … or short. Kids are quick to dive into a lesson or need some time to warm up to being together. Older kids might zip through an activity while their younger friends take a little longer.

Relax. We've got you covered.

You can use these sessions with kids in practically any setting: in Sunday school, children's church, evening programs, or while kids' parents are attending an adult class or small group. There's maximum flexibility because each session is written to last 45 minutes and then provides enough extras to fill a full hour. These sessions stretch to fit exactly what you need, when you need it. They're …

- **multi-aged**—suitable for mixed ages of elementary children;
- **easily adapted**—sessions work for just a couple kids or a packed classroom;
- **relational**—children grow close to Jesus *and* one another;
- **flexible**—brimming with options to fit varying time frames; and
- **fun**—even easily distracted kids will engage, learn, and grow.

So are you ready for some fun? Let's dive in!

How God Used
a Dove

The Point: God gives us hope.
Scripture Connect: Genesis 8:6–12

Supplies for all session 1 activities and options: plastic (or paper) cups, balloons, black plastic trash bag, stopwatch, Bible, paper, colored markers, propane candle lighter, smooth stones (1 per child)

The Basics for Leaders

Stuck.

That's how Noah felt on the ark because he was … well, stuck. As in water-all-around-no-land-in-sight stuck.

And Noah couldn't do anything about it except keep doing what he'd done all along: place his hope in God and trust that God would care for him, his family, and a boatload of animals.

In that way your kids have something in common with Noah—they're stuck too. Someone else sets their schedules, decides what they'll eat, and plans where they'll go on vacation.

But what they may *not* have in common with Noah is a deep trust in God. Heartfelt hope that God will care for and guide them.

You'll help your kids explore that hope through this session. And they'll discover that, no matter what, their hope is in God!

OPENING ACTIVITY—OPTION 1

TELL ME THUMBTHING

Time: about 5 minutes, depending on attendance
Supplies: none

After kids arrive, say: **When people like a movie, they sometimes give it a thumbs-up.** Demonstrate. **Really like the movie? Two thumbs-up. If they dislike or really dislike the movie, they give it one or two thumbs-down.** Demonstrate.

Please rate how this past week has gone for you. Was it a one or two thumbs-up week? A one or two thumbs-down week? Or maybe you'd give it one thumbs-up and one thumbs-down—it was a good *and* bad week.

Rate your week now.

After kids rate their weeks, give kids 30 seconds each to explain why they rated their weeks as they did. You'll go first, sharing a story that models the sort of brief, personal stories you hope kids will share too.

Children will express themselves more over time, and hearing their stories will help you adapt this session to make it even more relevant to your kids' lives.

OPENING ACTIVITY—OPTION 2

PRECISION PLUCK

Time: about 5 minutes
Supplies: plastic (or paper) cups (1 per child)

Give each child a cup. Ask children to stand and then place their cups, bottom side up, on the floor between their feet.

Ask kids to use the thumb and index finger on one hand to create a "pincher," as if their hands are claws. Then ask kids to bend over and pick up their cups using only their claws.

Repeat the activity three times, each time placing cups back between their feet.

Then ask kids to close their eyes and keep them closed.

Explain that, at your signal, they'll do what they've just done: bend over and, using their claws, pick up the cups. Two rules:

- They *must* keep their eyes closed as they do this. No peeking!
- They get to close their claw just *once*—no feeling around and then positioning their claw.

Before kids move, ask them to call out a number that reflects how hopeful they are they can pick up their cup in one try: five if they're sure they can do it, zero if they're sure they can't, or some number in between.

Have kids try the activity several times and then sit. Collect and remove the cups.

Say: **We're talking about hope today. When you have hope you expect something to happen—even if you're not sure when or how.**

Some of you had more hope than others that you could pick up a cup without looking. But if you practiced long enough, you could do it every time. I have confidence—and hope—in you!

We'll see how someone had hope in God, but first let's play a game I call Water, Water, Everywhere!

Amazing Animals Game

WATER, WATER, EVERYWHERE

Time: about 10 minutes
Supplies: balloons (1 per child), black plastic trash bag, stopwatch

Before children arrive, inflate the balloons and hide them in a black plastic trash bag in a corner.

Tell kids they'll each adopt a dove—one that looks a *lot* like a balloon.

Their doves have a problem: they're in the middle of the ocean and there's no place to land. The goal of the game is for each child to keep his or her dove in the air for 60 seconds.

Give each child a balloon. **Say: Your dove has one hope, and it's you! If you keep your dove in the air for 60 seconds, it can settle down safely on dry land. If your dove hits the floor before a minute has passed, it's bye-bye, birdie. Your dove is done.**

Kids can keep their balloons in the air by batting them with their hands, feet, heads, or elbows. If a child's balloon hits the ground before you call time, have that child quietly stand over the fallen balloon buddy.

Start your timer and yell, **Go!**

When a minute has passed, give fresh instructions. Same goal (keep balloons in the air) but new rules: kids can't touch their balloons. They can wave their arms or huff and puff to keep balloons flying—but no touching.

Say: **Your doves are counting on you to keep them flying for 20 seconds. Ready? Set? Go!**

When 20 seconds have passed, have kids return their balloons to you and then sit in a circle. Join them.

Ask:

- **What made this game easy or difficult?**
- **Your dove hoped you could keep it in the air. In real life, what do you hope you can do?**
- **Who do you hope comes through for you? What are you hoping that person will do?**

Say: **The man we're about to meet placed his hope in God, in a boat he'd built with his family, and in a dove. Let's meet Noah and that dove now.**

Amazing Animals Bible Story

FORTUNATELY, UNFORTUNATELY

Time: about 20 minutes
Supplies: Bible

Join your kids sitting in a circle.

Ask kids to show you—and one another—their best smiley face and then their best frowny face.

Ask kids to wear whatever face they think best fits each part of what you'll read aloud. When you pause, kids decide: smiley or frowny faces.

A man named Noah loved God. (pause) **He and his family were faithful to God.** (pause) **Nobody else loved God.** (pause) **God decided to flood the earth and sort of start over with his creation.** (pause) **God decided to save Noah and his family.** (pause) **They couldn't swim long enough to outlast the flood.** (pause) **Fortunately, God told them to build an ark—a huge, floating boat.** (pause) **The animals couldn't swim long enough either.** (pause) **There was room on the ark for lots of animals.** (pause) **The flood lasted for months, and then the ark settled on a mountain.** (pause) **When Noah could finally see mountaintops, he opened a window in the ark.** (pause)

Ask a willing reader to continue the account by reading aloud Genesis 8:6–12. No one willing? Then you can read the passage aloud yourself.

Ask:

- Noah sent a dove out three times. The first time, when the dove came back, how do you think Noah and his family felt? Why?
- How about the second time when the dove came back with the leaf of an olive tree? How do you think they felt then? Why?
- How about the third time when the dove didn't come back at all? If you were Noah, how would you feel? Why?

Thank children for sharing their answers. When kids participate, they're engaged, and they'll *stay* engaged if you thank them for sharing their thoughts.

Say: **Noah had hope he and his family would be able to leave the ark. When the dove came back carrying a leaf, it meant the dove had found dry land. When the dove didn't return at all, it meant the dove had found a place to build a nest.**

Noah's hope wasn't in the dove—it was in God. The dove just pointed to God's promise to give Noah and his family a new life after the flood passed.

Ask:

- **What promise has God made to you, in the Bible, you know he'll keep?** Help kids with suggestions as needed.
- **What points you toward that promise?**

Take your time helping kids discuss their answers to the question. Ask respectful follow-up questions like, "Why does that promise matter to you?" or "Why do you think you can believe that promise?" Or simply say, "Tell me more."

After your conversation, move to the Closing Prayer.

CLOSING PRAYER

ENEMY UPLIFT

Time: about 5 minutes
Supplies: plastic (or paper) cups (1 per child)

Ask kids to hold their cups in both hands with the open end of the cup facing up.

Say: **Let's take turns asking God to fill us up with hope.**

Encourage kids to take turns praying aloud, turning to God as the source of their hope.

Then ask kids to turn their cups so the open end of each cup is facing down.

Encourage kids to then take turns praying that God helps them pour hope into the lives of someone else by being kind … by being loving … by pointing others toward God.

Then briefly pray for each child by name.

EXTRA-TIME ACTIVITY–OPTION 1

HOPE MINI-POSTERS

Time: about 10 minutes
Supplies: paper, colored markers

Before kids arrive, make a sample poster that shows what you're hoping for and reminds you that God is the giver of your hope. Encourage kids to fill in their mini-posters with hopeful doodles, drawings, and words.

As kids work, talk about this:

• **What are you hoping will happen in your life?**

Encourage kids to take home their mini-posters to display where they'll be reminded: God is the giver of their hope!

Do you have kids who zipped through the activity? Have them make a second poster to give to a friend!

EXTRA-TIME ACTIVITY–OPTION 2

WET HEAD

Time: about 10 minutes
Supplies: water balloon, propane candle lighter

Before kids arrive fill a balloon with water and keep it and the candle lighter out of sight.

Ask for a volunteer to sit on a chair. Stand behind the chair and hold the balloon over the volunteer's head. Explain that you'll light a flame and let it touch the balloon—and see how long it takes for the balloon to burst.

Ask kids to guess: **Will it take three seconds? Ten seconds? Twenty seconds?**

After kids guess, light the flame and let it scorch the bottom of the balloon ... which won't burst. The heat of the flame is dissipated by the water.

After 30 seconds, turn off the flame and move the balloon.

Ask kids:

- **Were you hoping the balloon would or wouldn't burst? Why?**
- **When have you expected for something bad to happen—and it didn't happen?**

Say: **Sometimes what we expect to happen—doesn't. But when we expect God to keep a promise, we can have huge hope because God is always faithful. That's why God gives us hope!**

EXTRA-TIME ACTIVITY–OPTION 3

HOT STONES

Time: about 5 minutes
Supplies: smooth stones (1 per child), markers

Give each child a stone and a marker.

Explain that some people carry "worry stones" in their pockets to fidget with when they're worried. But if you have hope in God, there's no reason to worry—he's caring for you!

Ask kids to use markers to write or draw something about God on their stones. As they work, talk about this:

- **What's a place where you worry? What do you worry about there?**

Encourage kids to take their "hope stones" with them and, when they worry, to hold the stones to remind themselves: God gives us hope!

How God Used
Camels

The Point: God leads us.
Scripture Connect: Genesis 24:1–4, 9–27

Supplies for all session 2 activities and options: paper plates (inexpensive, uncoated ones; 5 per child), string, masking tape, stopwatch, Bible, several rolls of toilet paper

The Basics for Leaders

If you've ever felt at a loss about what to do next, you'll understand why Abraham's servant was worried.

Abraham had ordered him to pack up some camels with gifts, travel to a distant land, and pick out a wife for Abraham's son Isaac.

As plans go, that's a bit thin. What if Isaac didn't like her? What if she didn't like Isaac? If anything went wrong, guess who'd be out of a job?

So the servant begged God for guidance. He didn't want to choose the wife; he wanted *God* to do the choosing. He wanted to follow where *God* led him.

God answered the servant's prayer and led him to Rebekah—a great wife for Isaac. God's willing to lead you and your kids too. He'll guide you and help you make good choices.

That's the truth your kids will explore in this session. Thanks for helping them make that discovery!

OPENING ACTIVITY-OPTION 1

TELL ME THUMBTHING

Time: about 5 minutes, depending on attendance
Supplies: none

After kids arrive, say: **When people like a movie, they sometimes give it a thumbs-up.** Demonstrate. **Really like the movie? Two thumbs-up. If they dislike or really dislike the movie, they give it one or two thumbs-down.** Demonstrate.

Please rate how this past week has gone for you. Was it a one or two thumbs-up week? A one or two thumbs-down week? Or maybe you'd give it one thumbs-up and one thumbs-down—it was a good *and* bad week.

Rate your week now.

After kids rate their weeks, give kids 30 seconds each to explain why they rated their weeks as they did. You'll go first, sharing a story that models the sort of brief, personal stories you hope kids will share too.

Children will express themselves more over time, and hearing their stories will help you adapt this session to make it even more relevant to your kids' lives.

OPENING ACTIVITY-OPTION 2

FOLLOW MY LEAD

Time: about 5 minutes
Supplies: none

Ask kids to stand and form a circle so everyone can see everyone else.

Say: **Okay, I want everybody to follow my lead.**

Silently act out that you're climbing a ladder ... then digging a hole ... then painting a wall. Congratulate kids on doing as you did, letting you lead them.

Announce that kids will take turns doing something that everyone else will try too. It can be something simple, but it will be *way* more fun if kids show their superpowers—things they can do that others might not be able to do: handstands, touching one's nose with one's tongue, whistling, or ripping off 10 jumping jacks in record time.

Go around the circle, letting kids take turns leading one another. Then sit and discuss:

- **Which action was easiest to follow—and which was hardest for you?**
- **How did it feel to have everyone following you?**

Say: **Today we're talking about how God leads us. Of course, that only works if we're willing to be led and if we're willing to follow him. Just like it was your choice to follow other leaders just now, it's your choice whether you'll follow God where he leads you.**

I hope you will—because it's always someplace good. And when we lean on him for help, he never leads us to do something that's impossible ... like touching our noses with our tongues!

Before we see how God used some camels to help lead one man, let's play a game of Paper Plate Chase!

Amazing Animals Game

PAPER PLATE CHASE

Time: about 10 minutes
Supplies: paper plates (inexpensive, uncoated ones; 5 per child), string, masking tape, stopwatch

AGE-ALERT TIPS
Try to balance the two teams with both **younger** and **older children**.

Before children arrive, use string to define an open, rectangular playing area. Use strips of masking tape to keep the string in place. Be strategic about the rectangle. If you expect 10 kids, make it about as wide as five kids would be if they were standing side-by-side, arms out wide, hands clasped. You'll see why this matters when you play.

Form your kids into two teams—half on each team. Name the two teams Chasers and Dodgers.

Explain the rules: **Chasers will attempt to tag all the members of the Dodgers team but can only move by stepping on paper plates they toss on the ground. Give each Chaser 10 paper plates; Dodgers won't need any.**

Chasers can pick up plates from the ground and reuse them to keep moving.

Dodgers will try to avoid being tagged, but must stay within the string boundaries. If a Dodger is tagged, he or she becomes a Chaser.

Start Chasers out in one corner of the rectangle and start the Dodgers anywhere they want to be. Give Chasers two minutes to tag Dodgers, and then have teams change roles for another two-minute round.

But before the start of the second round, announce that you've received orders from Chaser High Command. The General has ordered Chasers to start at a narrow end of the rectangle, side-by-side, and advance in a line toward the other end. There won't be room for any Dodgers to dart past them.

After playing a second round, have kids pick up the paper plates and give them to you and then sit in a circle. Join them. Ask:

- Which did you enjoy most, being a Chaser or Dodger? Why?
- How was the second round of our game different from the first?

Say: In the second round the Chasers followed the lead of the Chaser High Command and that changed everything.

When we follow God's plan, it makes a huge difference too. Sometimes God spells his plan out in the Bible. And other times—well, other times it's like what a guy with a herd of camels experienced.

Let's hear about him now.

Amazing Animals Bible Story

INSTANT DRAMA

Time: about 20 minutes
Supplies: Bible

It's time for an instant drama! It works like this: assign kids the roles of characters who'll appear in what you read; and then as you read, have kids act out what happens in the story.

Pause often to allow time for actions, and if needed, give a bit of stage direction. But let this be organic; half the fun is kids figuring out how they'll act out the actions as they move around the room.

Assign these roles: Abraham, the servant, Rebekah, and the camels. If you have just a few children, double up roles or join in yourself. Lots of kids? Add more camels or toss in a few friends for Rebekah. Be sure everyone has a part and is actively engaged.

(Please note there's a tricky bit to navigate: Genesis 24:2 describes the servant putting his hand under the thigh of Abraham. Either skip over that detail or be ready to explain it. It was an ancient custom that apparently involved either holding the groin or letting someone sit on your hand. We suggest skipping it.)

Have fun! Add playful, action elements like "The servant piled gifts on the first camel, but the saddle slipped off" or "Then the servant remembered: camels spit."

Read through Genesis 24:1–4, 9–27. Then ask kids to join you in a circle to discuss:

- **Where did you see someone or something being led in this story?**
- **Tell about a time you followed a leader and things went well. Who was the leader and what happened?**
- **Tell about a time you followed a leader and things didn't go well. What happened?**
- **The people in this Bible account believed God was leading them. Do you think God helps people make big decisions in life today? Why or why not?**
- **What's a time you thought God was leading you?**

Say: **God leads us if we want him to and if we're willing to follow. Let's pray about where he might be leading us now.**

CLOSING PRAYER

PLATE PRAYERS
Time: about 5 minutes
Supplies: paper plates (1 per child)

Give each child a paper plate. Ask kids to stand in a tight circle—facing outward. Have them back up until they're huddled together, rubbing shoulders.

Say: **Sometimes it's scary to follow where God leads. We don't know how things will turn out. He may lead us to do hard things.**

Toss your plate onto the floor a few feet in front of you. (pause)

Right now we're close to our friends. It's easy to feel safe because someone's got our back. But here's the truth: God always has your back. He's always with you.

Take a step forward to stand on your plate. (pause)

Ask kids to stand, silently, for 30 seconds and consider what steps God might want them to take as they follow him. Since they know God wants them to be kind, maybe they could befriend a new kid at school or in the neighborhood. Since they know God wants them to know him better, maybe they could begin reading the Bible every day. They could help a parent who is ill by praying for that parent.

Offer some cues as you see fit. Ask kids to silently consider following God's leading.

After 30 seconds wrap up by saying "amen."

Before kids move, ask them to remember anything that came to mind while they were quiet—and to try and act on those things this week.

EXTRA-TIME ACTIVITY—OPTION 1

INSTANT IMPERSONATIONS

Time: about 10 minutes

Supplies: none

Here's some instant letting-others-lead-you practice!

Have kids stand and form a circle. Stand in the middle and explain that you'll call out an animal or object and everyone will have until you count to 10—and you'll count super fast—to impersonate that animal or object.

AGE-ALERT TIPS

Be sensitive to **younger children**—give them more obvious, familiar animals or objects.

After several rounds, pick someone else to stand in the circle and lead. Join kids in doing impersonations.

A few words you might call out: monkey, vacuum cleaner, tiger, helicopter, elephant, mosquito, pogo stick.

Rotate kids through the center of the circle, then return to the center yourself.

Call out a few things God might lead kids to do: **Be kind. Share your faith. Give to others.**

Then have kids sit and talk together about how they can follow God's leading. Ask:

• What does being kind look and sound like? How about sharing your faith and giving to others?

EXTRA-TIME ACTIVITY-OPTION 2

CAMEL TRAIN

Time: about 5 minutes
Supplies: none

Say: **Getting 10 camels to all go the same direction—that must have been a challenge for Abraham's servant. Let's see how that might work.**

Ask kids to stand in a single-file row and to then bend over and grab the ankles of the person in front of them. They're now a camel train!

Describe for them their journey from Abraham's home to the well where Rebekah gave them water. Give them directions to move forward … backward … even sideways.

Have fun!

EXTRA-TIME ACTIVITY-OPTION 3

BEAUTIFUL BRIDE

Time: about 10 minutes
Supplies: several rolls of toilet paper

Say: **Rachel must have been a beautiful bride when she married Isaac. We don't know for sure how brides dressed in Abraham's day, but maybe she wore a white dress.**

Explain that you'll all work together to create a beautiful bridal dress and veil—out of toilet paper.

Ask for a volunteer to be Rachel.

Give kids several rolls of toilet paper and have them do their best to create a wedding-worthy dress and veil. Encourage them to talk as they work together, following one another's suggestions on how to accomplish their mission.

Note: While this will certainly be a photo-worthy endeavor, don't start snapping photos and uploading to social media. Take photos, but send them to a parent of your Rachel—that parent can decide whether it's something to share with the world.

How God Used

Quail

The Point: God hears our prayers.
Scripture Connect: Numbers 11:18–20, 31–32

Supplies for all session 3 activities and options: plastic cups, spoons (1 per child), dried beans (10 per child), straws (2 per child), cotton balls, stopwatch, Bible, electric drill (or small Phillips-head screwdriver), string cut in 12' lengths (1 per pair of kids), scissors, paper clips, clear tape, candy kisses (2 per child)

The Basics for Leaders

Uh-oh.

Soon after God's people were safely out of Egypt, heading for the Promised Land, they started complaining to Moses about not having meat to eat.

God was not amused. In fact, he was angry.

The complaints showed zero gratitude for what God did and was doing for his people, and even less initiative. They could have hunted for wildlife or slaughtered an occasional sheep, but instead they complained about how God was treating them.

Today you'll help kids notice that, though people complained to Moses, God heard them. God knew their hearts and thoughts just as he knows ours.

Not only did God hear the unspoken prayers of his people; he responded. Just not in the way they expected.

God heard the prayers of his people in the wilderness–and he hears the prayers of your kids too.

And he *will* respond!

25

OPENING ACTIVITY—OPTION 1

TELL ME THUMBTHING

Time: about 5 minutes, depending on attendance
Supplies: none

After kids arrive, say: **When people like a movie, they sometimes give it a thumbs-up.** Demonstrate. **Really like the movie? Two thumbs-up. If they dislike or really dislike the movie, they give it one or two thumbs-down.** Demonstrate.

Please rate how this past week has gone for you. Was it a one or two thumbs-up week? A one or two thumbs-down week? Or maybe you'd give it one thumbs-up and one thumbs-down—it was a good *and* bad week.

Rate your week now.

After kids rate their weeks, give kids 30 seconds each to explain why they rated their weeks as they did. You'll go first, sharing a story that models the sort of brief, personal stories you hope kids will share too.

Children will express themselves more over time, and hearing their stories will help you adapt this session to make it even more relevant to your kids' lives.

OPENING ACTIVITY—OPTION 2

BEAN LAUNCH

Time: about 5 minutes
Supplies: plastic cups, spoons (1 per child), dried beans (10 per child)

Give each child a spoon and 10 beans. Place a cluster of cups together, open end up, about 10 feet from the kids.

Explain that the kids' goal is to get their beans into a cup by placing the bean in the bowl of the spoon and then flipping the handle to launch the bean. Demonstrate how to do it. It's okay if you miss the cups—you'll be giving kids the okay to be equally bad bean launchers!

After kids make 10 attempts, you can either gather up the spoons or let them go pick up beans and try again.

Once you've finished launching, have kids sit in a circle. Join them and ask:

- Did you get better at launching beans as you went, or worse? Why?
- If you were telling someone else how to launch beans, what tips would you share?

Say: **Today we're talking about prayer—and how God hears our prayers.** Launching a prayer isn't exactly like launching a bean, but they have this in common: practice helps you get more comfortable with both.

That's why we'll practice praying today. And we'll find out something about prayer that you might not know.

But first, a game of Corral the Quail!

Amazing Animals Game

CORRAL THE QUAIL
Time: about 5 minutes
Supplies: plastic cups (1 per child), straws (2 per child), cotton balls, stopwatch

Give each child a plastic cup and two straws.

Say: **When God's people were on their way to the Promised Land, they complained that they didn't have any meat to eat. God sent about a zillion quail—little birds—that the people could pluck and eat.**

They filled baskets with the quail … like you're about to do!

Recruit a child to help you scatter cotton balls all around the room. As you litter, explain that, at your signal, kids will use their straws to pick up as many cotton balls as they can, as quickly as they can.

They can try to spear cotton balls, suck up the balls using the straws, or use straws as chopsticks. What they *can't* do is touch the cotton balls. Tell kids they have 60 seconds to gather up all their fluffy white quail, starting … now!

After one minute has passed, have kids gather up the rest of the cotton balls by hand and sit with you in a circle.

Ask:

- **What's your favorite food?**
- **When you get to eat your favorite food, how do you feel?**

- How much of that favorite food would you have to eat before you never wanted to eat it again?

Say: **God's people had a food they missed as they marched toward the Promised Land: meat. So they complained ... and God heard them.**

God answered their complaints because God doesn't just hear our prayers; he answers them too. He just didn't answer their prayers in the way his people expected!

Amazing Animals Bible Story

THE GOOD OLD DAYS

Time: about 20 minutes
Supplies: Bible

Join your kids sitting in a circle.

Tell kids the Israelites were missing the "good old days" of being in Egypt. But when people talk about the "good old days," they sometimes forget what those good old days were really like. Yes, when Grandpa was 20 years old, he didn't have as many aches and pains. But maybe he was also in the army and people were shooting at him.

Say: **We're joining God's people on their way to the Promised Land. God has led them out of Egypt. But instead of being grateful, they're complaining that they have no meat to eat. They're talking about the good old days in Egypt when they had plenty of meat for dinner.**

Explain that, before you read about how God answered their complaints, you want kids to talk about their *own* "good old days."

Share this example: **In the good old days when I was a baby, people did everything for me and I could just relax. But ... I also had to wear diapers. And I couldn't talk. And I didn't have any teeth. Maybe those days weren't so good after all!**

Ask kids to finish these "good old days" with examples from their own lives:

- When you were at the beach, you got to go swimming, but ...
- When you went to school, you got to see friends, but ...
- When school was canceled because of snow or for another reason, you got to sleep in, but ...

Say: **When God's people were in Egypt, they were slaves. They worked all the time and couldn't worship God freely. But they sort of forgot all that because they wanted meat for dinner. And God heard them.**

Read aloud Numbers 11:18–20, 31–32 and then talk about this:

- **God seems sort of … upset. Why do you think he was upset with his people?**
- **The people were complaining to Moses. How do you think God knew what was in the hearts and minds of the whiners?**
- **How does it feel knowing that God knows what's in your heart and mind?**

Say: **Thanks for sharing what you think. I love that we get to talk together! It's true that God answers our prayers—sometimes when we don't even say those prayers out loud.**

He's with us, always.

He pays attention to us, always.

He answers us, always.

Let's pray in a way that maybe you've never prayed before. Ready?

CLOSING PRAYER

LISTENING IN PRAYER

Time: about 5 minutes
Supplies: none

Ask kids to form pairs and move in the room so they can talk easily with their partners. Ask kids to tell their partners about something in their lives with which they could use God's help.

You'll go first. Share an appropriate concern in your life. Say: **Your turn. Tell your partner how you could use God's help. Maybe it's at school, at home, or with a friend or family member.**

After kids talk for several minutes, get their attention and say "amen."

Explain that, as they shared with their partner, God was listening in too.

EXTRA-TIME ACTIVITY-OPTION 1

LONG-DISTANCE CALL

Time: about 10 minutes
Supplies: plastic cups (1 per child), electric drill (or small Phillips-head screwdriver), string cut in 12' lengths (1 per pair of kids), scissors, paper clips, clear tape

> ### AGE-ALERT TIPS
> **Younger children** may need help with this project. Pair them with **older kids**.

Before kids arrive, cut the string and create a small hole in the bottom of one plastic cup per child.

Ask kids to form pairs, and give each child a cup, paper clip, and access to tape. Give each pair a length of string. Explain that partners will stick one end of their string through each of their cups, tie the string ends to paper clips, and then tape the paper clips to the inside bottom of their cups. Then they'll slowly walk apart, each of them holding a cup, until the string is taut. Since it's tied to a paper clip, the string won't pull back through the holes.

Ask kids to take turns speaking softly into their cups while their partners place their cups over one of their ears. Voices vibrate along the string and make it possible to hear what's being said.

Have kids trade answers with their partners to these questions:

- **What's someplace you'd like to go that you've never been before?**
- **If you had to eat a spider or a fly, which would you pick? Why?**
- **How much money do you need to have to feel rich?**

Have partners come back together and sit in a circle. Ask:

- **If you could say just one thing to God, what would it be?**

Take turns saying those things to God in prayer.

EXTRA-TIME ACTIVITY—OPTION 2

KISS ON YOUR FOREHEAD

Time: about 5 minutes
Supplies: candy kisses (2 per child)

Explain that because the Israelites had a challenge collecting food, you'll give your kids a challenge too.

Have kids each unwrap a candy kiss and then lean back so they're staring straight up at the ceiling. Once they're in position, they'll place a candy kiss on their foreheads and then try to get the candy into their mouths without touching it with their hands.

If candy hits the floor, the five-second rule applies—pick it up and try again. And yes, you *must* unwrap the candy (when foil-wrapped candy hits a dental filling it's a memorable, painful experience).

Give kids a second piece of candy to enjoy together as you discuss:

- **The Israelites probably couldn't look at a quail again without remembering that God answers our prayers. What reminds you that God answers your prayers?**

EXTRA-TIME ACTIVITY—OPTION 3

LISTENING TOO

Time: about 5 minutes
Supplies: none

Say: **Prayer isn't just us telling God what we want. It's a time to thank him, to be sorry for doing wrong, and more. And when we pray, it's a good time to remember things he has told (or promised) us in the Bible. God has important things we need to listen to. So we listen to him through the Bible, and he lets us talk to him in prayer.**

Ask kids to spread out around the room and to pray silently to God.

After a few minutes, say: **Thanks for listening to us, God. Please help us do a good job of listening to you too. Amen.**

How God Used
Balaam's Donkey

The Point: God uses us.
Scripture Connect: Numbers 22:21–34

Supplies for all session 4 activities and options: slips of paper, pencil, stopwatch, plastic cups (1 per 3 children), string (1 length of 12" per child), rubber bands, sink (or bucket), water (or flour or packing peanuts), Bible, name stickers (optional), index cards (1 per child plus extras), scissors, markers, tape, old newspapers

The Basics for Leaders

Kids hear this a lot: wait.

Want to watch that movie? Wait until you're older. Want to ride the roller coaster? Wait until you're taller.

Want to serve God?

Ah–for that there's no waiting. Your kids are ready right now.

God wants to use *all* his people to serve others, encourage one another, and praise him–and that includes children. If they're willing, God can use them in powerful ways.

You'll help your kids discover that truth as you consider "someone" else God used: a talking donkey.

The God who used a donkey to change a prophet's world is certainly able to use every child you serve in a powerful way too.

OPENING ACTIVITY—OPTION 1

TELL ME THUMBTHING

Time: about 5 minutes, depending on attendance
Supplies: none

After kids arrive, say: **When people like a movie, they sometimes give it a thumbs-up.** Demonstrate. **Really like the movie? Two thumbs-up. If they dislike or really dislike the movie, they give it one or two thumbs-down.** Demonstrate.

Please rate how this past week has gone for you. Was it a one or two thumbs-up week? A one or two thumbs-down week? Or maybe you'd give it one thumbs-up and one thumbs-down—it was a good *and* bad week.

Rate your week now.

After kids rate their weeks, give kids 30 seconds each to explain why they rated their weeks as they did. You'll go first, sharing a story that models the sort of brief, personal stories you hope kids will share too.

Children will express themselves more over time, and hearing their stories will help you adapt this session to make it even more relevant to your kids' lives.

OPENING ACTIVITY—OPTION 2

TONGUE TWISTERS

Time: about 5 minutes
Supplies: slips of paper, pencil, stopwatch

Before kids arrive, print each of these tongue twisters on a separate slip of paper:

- Sally sells seashells by the seashore.
- Leslie's lovely lemon liniment lingers.
- Rubber baby buggy bumpers.
- Double bubble gum bubbles double.
- Chad cheerily cheers cheesy cheese.

AGE-ALERT TIPS

Allow **younger children** who are aren't comfortable readers to take a pass if they want—or to say the "rubber baby buggy bumpers" line. It's the easiest!

Ask kids to stand, and then lead them in doing a few jumping jacks, plus a stretch or two. Explain that, now that you're warmed up, you'll all give a workout to a muscle that's often overlooked in workouts: your tongues.

The goal: for each child to read one of the tongue twisters aloud three times in a row: once at a slow speed, then a normal speed, then at super-deluxe-zoomer speed. You'll time all three efforts and see if kids can speak faster without making more mistakes. Have fun with this. There are no college fast-talking scholarships at stake.

You'll go first. Your stumbles will help kids relax if they can't quite master a terribly twisty tongue twister too. (Read *that* five times fast!)

Once everyone has had a turn, ask kids to join you in a circle and do this:

- Tell about a time that something you said got you into trouble.

Start by sharing your own age-appropriate story. After several kids have shared, say: **Today we'll hear how what someone said got him into trouble—but God used his words to save someone's life. Which is amazing because that person had never spoken before. And he wasn't really a person—he was *a donkey*.**

More about that later. Right now, let's play a game of Band Together!

Amazing Animals Game

BAND TOGETHER

Time: about 10 minutes
Supplies: plastic cups (1 per 3 children), string (1 length of 12" per child), scissors, rubber bands (1 around each cup), sink (or bucket), water (or flour or packing peanuts)

Before kids arrive, cut the string and place a rubber band around each cup. Be sure they fit snuggly. Tie a length of string to the rubber band on three "sides" of the cup—spaced so lifting all three strings at the same time will keep the cup stable as it rises.

This game is more fun if you add an inch of water to each cup, but it *will* be spilled so plan accordingly. (In a carpeted area? Add something that's easy to vacuum up instead of water: packing peanuts or flour.)

Say: **Today we'll talk about how God uses us. Sometimes when he uses us, he has us work together—so let's practice that now.**

Form kids into groups of three and give each group a cup. Their job: Place the cup on the floor and then have each person take one of the strings. When you give the word, they're to lift the cup using only the strings, carry it to the sink, and empty the cup. They can—and should—talk as they work together, but at no time can they touch their cups with their hands.

Sounds easy, but … well, you'll see.

Try this several times so kids can learn as they go. Then collect the cups, clean up any spilled water, and sit in a circle to discuss:

- **What made it hard or easy to work together?**
- **What's something you've done with others that you never could have done on your own?**

Say: **God uses his people to do amazing things—but he also uses animals to do amazing things. Let's see what God did through a donkey owned by a man named Balaam.**

Amazing Animals Bible Story

SOUND EFFECTS

Time: about 15 minutes
Supplies: Bible

Tell kids they'll help you read a passage from the Bible by providing sound effects. Assign the following roles. If you have a lot of kids, assign one role to more than one child. Very few kids? Give multiple roles to a child or two.

- Donkey: Say, "Talking donkey here!"
- Balaam: Say, "Comin' through!"
- Angel of the Lord: Say, "Ta-da!"
- Balaam's Foot: Say, "Ouch!"

Have kids practice calling out their character's line several times.

Tell kids you're like an orchestra conductor—you'll signal when different characters should jump in with their lines. It won't be every time a character's name is mentioned, so kids should stay alert and keep an eye on you.

Read aloud Numbers 22:21–34, pausing often to lift an index finger to cue one character or another. Make a *huge* deal out of cuing Balaam's Foot–that actor appears just once.

When you've finished reading, talk about this:

- Why do you think God had the donkey talk?
- In what ways did God use the character you played in this story?

Once you and your kids have talked, say: **I think God wanted to get Balaam's attention. When Balaam's donkey spoke up … mission accomplished! God used the donkey and God wants to use us too. You, me, all of us.**

Ask:

- Where or when in your life might you have the chance to speak up for God? To tell someone about Jesus or to just step in and help people get along?

After kids talk about that, move along to the prayer time.

CLOSING PRAYER

USED BY GOD PRAYER
Time: about 5 minutes
Supplies: name stickers (optional)

Ask kids to sit in a circle.

Go around the circle, calling each child by name and then affirming that child.

If you have lots of kids and you worry about remembering names, have kids wear name stickers at this session. *It's very important that you call each child by name.*

An alternate method: As you go around the circle, have all children introduce themselves by name as each child says, "My name is _____, and I want God to use me."

You can follow by saying, "_____, God is already using you. I see …"

Give each child a specific affirmation about how you've seen God use that child in the context of this session. Some options might include these:

- I've seen you be patient when we were moving the cups of water. God can use your patience.
- I've seen you bring laughter to this room, brightening our day. God can use your humor.
- I've seen you jump in to help others. God can use your caring heart.

When you've made your way around the circle, wrap up by thanking God for how he's already using each child. Ask God to continue using you all.

EXTRA-TIME ACTIVITY-OPTION 1

INDEX CARD PUPPET SKITS

Time: about 10 minutes
Supplies: index cards, scissors, markers, stopwatch

Before kids arrive cut two holes in each index card as shown. You'll need one card per child, with a few extras on hand just in case.

Give each child a card and access to a few markers. Explain that kids will each stick their index finger and middle finger of one hand through the holes to be the legs of their puppets. Their job is to draw a self-portrait above the legs.

It'll help if you draw yourself to show as an example.

Say: **You can draw a stick figure, a full portrait worthy of a frame, or anything in between. But you'll have just two minutes to do the deed. And use the blank side of the index card unless having the lines is helpful to you.**

When kids have finished, it's time for show-and-tell. Have kids take turns introducing their puppet look-alikes.

Ask kids to form pairs, and give each pair this assignment: **Take two minutes to come up with a situation you can act out with your puppets. The situation should be one in which one of them gets to be used by God to help the other person.**

They'll act out their situations by using their puppets and talking.

After two minutes of prep time have passed, have each pair premiere their puppet skit. When they've all finished, applaud wildly, encourage your actors, and then have kids discuss this:

- **How does it feel when you know God is using you to help others?**
- **Why do you think you feel the way you feel?**

When kids are done talking, say: **You don't have to wait to become a grown-up before God can use you in a wonderful way. God uses us—all of us!**

EXTRA-TIME ACTIVITY–OPTION 2

DONKEY CONSTRUCTION

Time: about 10 minutes
Supplies: tape, old newspapers, stopwatch

Tell kids you need one volunteer for every five kids in the room. Once your volunteers have been identified, ask them to get on their hands and knees. Then announce: **Congratulations! You're about to be transformed into ... donkeys.**

Have a team of four other kids gather around each volunteer and, at your signal, spend four minutes using tape and newspaper to transform their volunteer into a donkey by adding ears, a snout, a newspaper coat, a tail ... whatever helps.

Don't supply scissors; kids can rip the newspaper pages.

To keep kids on pace, call out when time reaches the two-minute and one-minute mark. When time is up, have everyone but the donkeys step back and admire their work.

If you have just a few kids, volunteer to be donkey-ized yourself and let them work as a team.

Wrap up by inviting the donkeys to speak. Say: **You're not just donkeys— you're talking donkeys. Anything you'd like to say?**

Have kids un-decorate their volunteers and collect the newspaper for recycling.

EXTRA-TIME ACTIVITY–OPTION 3

USEFUL

Time: about 5 minutes
Supplies: stopwatch

Form kids into pairs and ask them to take two minutes to look around the room and find an object they can turn into something else—without hurting the object.

For instance, the sturdy cushion of a chair could become a punching bag. A light bulb can be a sock stretcher. Tell kids to be creative, and then once the two minutes have ended, have pairs do a show-and-tell.

Say: **Sometimes when God uses us, he uses us in ways we never expected. Maybe you plan to grow up and be a doctor and help people. Fine—but God can use you right now to help your elderly neighbors rake their leaves or shovel snow off their sidewalk.**

Be looking for ways God can use you!

How God Used
Lions

The Point: God is faithful.
Scripture Connect: Daniel 6:1–23

Supplies for all session 5 activities and options: blindfolds (1 per every 2 children), plastic cups (1 per child), marshmallows (1 per pair), Bible, stopwatch

The Basics for Leaders

Faithful. Trustworthy. Loyal. Steadfast. Dependable.

For some of your kids, there's not much of that happening.

Grown-ups in their lives make promises that aren't—or can't be—kept. They offer assurances that turn out to be meaningless.

Kids wonder who they can really trust, who won't let them down, who's really faithful.

In this session you'll help your kids discover that God is always on that list. That no matter what's happening in their lives, he's faithful to walk through it with them. To stand beside them. To lead them.

Trustworthy. That's God.

OPENING ACTIVITY-OPTION 1

TELL ME THUMBTHING
Time: about 5 minutes, depending on attendance
Supplies: none

After kids arrive, say: **When people like a movie, they sometimes give it a thumbs-up.** Demonstrate. **Really like the movie? Two thumbs-up. If they dislike or really dislike the movie, they give it one or two thumbs-down.** Demonstrate.

Please rate how this past week has gone for you. Was it a one or two thumbs-up week? A one or two thumbs-down week? Or maybe you'd give it one thumbs-up and one thumbs-down—it was a good *and* **bad week.**

Rate your week now.

After kids rate their weeks, give kids 30 seconds each to explain why they rated their weeks as they did. You'll go first, sharing a story that models the sort of brief, personal stories you hope kids will share too.

Children will express themselves more over time, and hearing their stories will help you adapt this session to make it even more relevant to your kids' lives.

OPENING ACTIVITY—OPTION 2

TUGBOAT

Time: about 5 minutes
Supplies: blindfolds (1 per every 2 children)

Have kids form pairs, and while one child in each pair is blindfolding the other, create an obstacle course in the room by moving chairs and other objects.

Explain that the sighted child in each pair is a tugboat—guiding his or her partner to safely navigate the obstacle course by using these signals: a tap on the right shoulder for turning right; a tap on the left shoulder for a left turn; and a tap between the shoulders for a full, immediate stop.

Say: **There's no talking, but because tugboats blow whistles, feel free to whistle. Tugboats, stand behind your friends and let's see how you do.**

After all pairs have completed the course, have kids switch roles, and while blindfolds are being applied, rearrange the course. Then have pairs make their ways back to the starting line.

After this experience have kids discuss:

- **How hard or easy was it for you not to peek? Why?**
- **How much did you trust your tugboat? Why?**

Say: **It's sometimes hard to trust people. You don't believe they'll really do what they say they'll do. But you can always trust God. God is faithful—he keeps all his promises. And you can trust him to guide your steps in life because he sees things you don't see.**

We'll look at how God was faithful to someone who was in a lot of trouble, but first let's play a game of Faithful Cup Catch!

Amazing Animals Game

FAITHFUL CUP CATCH

Time: about 5 minutes
Supplies: plastic cups (1 per child), marshmallows (1 per pair)

Ask children to form pairs. Give each child a cup and each pair a marshmallow.

Ask the oldest person in each pair to line up against the wall. Partners will face one another, standing about a foot apart.

Explain that partners will toss their marshmallow back and forth, always catching it in a cup. After the first successful catch, partners will shout, "One!" And the partner not standing against the wall will take a giant step backward. When the marshmallow is caught again, the partners will shout, "Two!" Then another step backward.

You get the idea.

When partners get to "Twelve!," they'll be far apart, and a successful catch is worthy of a victory dance.

Dropped marshmallows can be picked up and the game resumed. Perfection isn't required; faithfulness to the task is!

When most pairs have finished, ask kids to join you sitting.

Say: **Who got it right every time? You never missed a catch?**

If a pair was perfect, lead a round of applause. But point out that at 50, 100, or 1,000 steps, there would have been a fail. No one's always perfect, but we can all be faithful.

Say: **Something was faithful all through this game: gravity. Missed marshmallows all fell down—every time. We can trust gravity. It's faithful.**

There's something else—someone else—we can always trust too. Someone who's faithful, no matter what. That's what our friend Daniel discovered.

Let's join him now.

Amazing Animals **Bible Story**

LION LUNCH INSTANT DRAMA

Time: about 20 minutes
Supplies: Bible

In this drama there won't be any audience—only participants! Assign these roles: King, Daniel, and Lions. Clear a space in the room to be your stage.

Say: **As I read this Bible account, act out your parts with flair. Maybe a Hollywood agent is watching!**

Some background: wicked advisers of King Darius got a law passed that nobody could pray to God. But Daniel faithfully prayed, so the king—who was even a friend of Daniel's!—tossed Daniel into a den of hungry lions.

Actors, take your places!

Read aloud Daniel 6:16–23. Pause often to give actors time to act out their roles. Add details as you go, telling the lions to roar with their mouths shut, or circle left or right. Have the king toss and turn on his bed. Be creative!

When the play has ended, applaud wildly and then, together, discuss:

- **Daniel was faithful—he kept talking with God. In what ways do you show that you're faithful to God?**
- **God was faithful to Daniel, but what if God hadn't saved Daniel from the lions? Would God still be faithful?**
- **The rule said Daniel couldn't pray. He had to obey the rule or obey God. What's a rule that might make you choose between obeying God and the rule?**

Say: **God never promised to protect Daniel from the lions ... or from sickness or from breaking a tooth. God doesn't promise us those things either.**

He promises to walk with us through whatever happens, and he promises eternal life to those who love and follow Jesus.

God always keeps his promises!

CLOSING PRAYER

PAUSE PRAYER
Time: about 5 minutes
Supplies: none

Ask kids to sit in different places in the room, with plenty of space between them, and to get into a non-fidgety posture. Explain that you'll lead them in a prayer that has pauses in it so they can quietly or silently talk to God about the things you bring up.

We suggest 20-second pauses, but you can adjust the timing for the age and wiring of your kids.

Pray: **God, thank you for being faithful. For always keeping your promises.**

What's a promise God has made to you in the Bible? Tell him what that promise is, and how you feel about it. (pause)

God, thank you that you help us be faithful too. Ask God how you could be more faithful to him. (pause)

God, thank you for people in our lives we can trust. Name someone you trust, and thank God for that person. (pause)

God, help us know you better and love you more deeply. If you love God, tell him why. If you don't yet love God, tell him why. (pause)

God, open our hearts to you. Amen.

EXTRA-TIME ACTIVITY—OPTION 1

COUNT ON ME
Time: about 10 minutes
Supplies: none

Help your kids get to know one another—and you—by taking turns filling in these blanks:

- I always ___.
- I never ___.

- I'll always say yes to ___.
- I'll always say no to ___.
- I'm always scared when I see ___.
- Something that always makes me sad is ___.
- I'm always happy when I see ___.

Share your own answers too, and ask follow-up questions when your kids share theirs.

Say: **You may think you'll never change your answers, but that might happen as you grow older. You're always happy to see kittens now; but if you develop an allergy to them, you'll be less happy around kittens.**

We do lots of changing—but God doesn't. He's the same now as he was in the past and will be in the future. That's one reason he's always faithful.

Another reason is that he loves you!

EXTRA-TIME ACTIVITY–OPTION 2

LION FACTS

Time: about 5 minutes
Supplies: none

Tell kids you'll share 10 facts about lions.

Say: **If you think what I say is true, roar. If you think I'm a lyin' lion, stay quiet.**

> FACT 1: **In dry places lions don't have to find water. They get enough water from eating plants and other animals.** (T)
> FACT 2: **A group of lions is called a pack.** (F—It's called a pride.)
> FACT 3: **Lions are bigger than tigers.** (F)
> FACT 4: **Lions often live up to 50 years.** (F—In the wild they average 12 years, in captivity up to 25 years.)
> FACT 5: **Lions are great swimmers.** (T)
> FACT 6: **Lions seldom sleep.** (F—They can sleep up to 22 hours per day.)
> FACT 7: **A lion is often called the King of the Jungle.** (T)
> FACT 8: **King of the Jungle is an accurate name.** (F—Most lions live in grasslands, not jungle.)
> FACT 9: **Female lions do most of the hunting.** (T)

FACT 10: A male lion's roar can be heard a mile away (T and F: It can be heard up to five miles away).

Say: **I'm not always trustworthy when it comes to telling you about lions. But God's always faithful when he tells us about himself—and us.**
Discuss:

- **What's something God has said about himself that you're glad is true?**
- **What's something he's said about you that you're glad is true?**

EXTRA-TIME ACTIVITY–OPTION 3

SLEEPING LIONS

Time: about 5 minutes
Supplies: stopwatch

Before kids arrive, remove or cover all wall clocks.

Ask kids to sit in a circle and to stick any cell phones or watches in their pockets.

Explain that kids are now all sleeping lions who'll only be able to munch a gazelle for lunch if they leap into action at precisely the right time. You'll tell them how many seconds to let go by before they leap to their feet. Whoever is closest to the exact time gets the gazelle.

Play three rounds: 18 seconds, 41 seconds, and 77 seconds. Ask kids to sit in a circle and discuss:

- **A good watch is faithful—it always shows the right time. Some of you weren't faithful time-tellers. What got in the way?**
- **How is that like or unlike what gets in the way of our being faithful in other ways?**

How God Used
a Great Fish

The Point: God gives us second chances.
Scripture Connect: Jonah 1:1–2:6; 3:1–3

Supplies for all session 6 activities and options: metal spoons, cheese puffs (or another inexpensive, tossable snack), Bible, blanket, 2 sheets of paper and a pencil per child, stopwatch, hat, index cards, pen

The Basics for Leaders

Some say that God is the God of second chances. Which isn't quite true.

Yes, God gives second chances to those who ask for them. And third chances. And thirty-third chances. It's called forgiveness and is something we all need—including your children.

Jonah had plenty of time to consider his need for a second chance while sitting in the belly of a great fish. And when he got that second chance, he made the most of it—he abandoned his fear and selfishness and obeyed God instead.

You'll give your kids the chance to consider second chances in this session, and you'll have the opportunity to talk with God about second chances in your life too.

OPENING ACTIVITY-OPTION 1

TELL ME THUMBTHING
Time: about 5 minutes, depending on attendance
Supplies: none

After kids arrive, say: **When people like a movie, they sometimes give it a thumbs-up.** Demonstrate. **Really like the movie? Two thumbs-up. If they dislike or really dislike the movie, they give it one or two thumbs-down.** Demonstrate.

Please rate how this past week has gone for you. Was it a one or two thumbs-up week? A one or two thumbs-down week? Or maybe you'd give it one thumbs-up and one thumbs-down—it was a good *and* bad week.

Rate your week now.

After kids rate their weeks, give kids 30 seconds each to explain why they rated their weeks as they did. You'll go first, sharing a story that models the sort of brief, personal stories you hope kids will share too.

Children will express themselves more over time, and hearing their stories will help you adapt this session to make it even more relevant to your kids' lives.

OPENING ACTIVITY–OPTION 2

SECOND-CHANCE PUFF LAUNCH

Time: about 5 minutes
Supplies: metal spoons, cheese puffs (or another inexpensive, tossable snack)

Give each child a spoon and two cheese puffs. Explain that the goal of this game is to place a cheese puff on the spoon and then toss the puff into the air, where it can be caught in the mouth of the child who launched the puff.

Say: **The five-second rule is in effect; if you miss the puff, pick it up and give it another try. See how few tries it takes for you to catch both puffs.**

After most kids have caught both puffs, have kids form pairs. Give them each two more puffs and have them launch puffs for their partners to catch in their mouths. Then let kids eat any remaining puffs as they sit together and discuss:

- **What helped you be successful as a puff launcher? What got in the way?**

- How well do you think this would work with spaghetti? Why?

Say: **You had lots of second chances in this game—and most of us needed them. Third and fourth chances too!**

Today we'll meet a guy who was happy to get a second chance. But first let's play a game of Spoon-arama!

Amazing Animals Game

SPOON-ARAMA

Time: about 5 minutes
Supplies: spoons (1 per child)

Ask kids to line up side by side along one wall and to each practice balancing their spoons on one finger. When they've each found that sweet spot, explain that they'll all walk to the opposite wall, touch it, and then turn around and come back—all without dropping their spoons.

If a spoon should drop, it's okay to stop, pick it up, and then continue.

Say: **You might not know it, but spoon racing is about to become an Olympic event. Here's your chance to show your skills!**

Have kids run the event three times: once as described above, then while walking backward, and then while on hands and knees (well, *hand* and knees).

Crank up the excitement by doing a play-by-play as kids participate. Speak in an excited-sportscaster voice and encourage kids along the way.

After the game has ended, sit with kids and talk about the following:

- **How helpful was it to have a second, third, or fourth chance? Why?**
- **Tell about some other time you were given a second chance.**

Tell an age-appropriate story from your life first to get the ball rolling and to model what you're looking for from the kids.

Honor kids' stories by listening carefully and thanking kids for sharing.

Say: **I'm grateful for second chances I've been given, but someone who was even more grateful was Jonah.**

Let's talk about him now.

Amazing Animals Bible Story

FISH FOOD INSTANT DRAMA

Time: about 20 minutes
Supplies: Bible, blanket

Assign these roles to your kids: Jonah, the captain, and the sailors. The rest of your kids will play the part of wicked people. Just a few kids? One sailor will work, and you can play all the wicked people yourself.

Explain that you'll read Jonah 1:1–17 aloud, pausing often so kids have time to act out the action described in the Bible's account of Jonah's adventure. When you get to the part about Jonah being swallowed, cover Jonah with the blanket.

When you finish reading, ask Jonah to stay covered. Have the rest of your actors sit next to the blanketed Jonah as you share the rest of the story (based on Jonah 2:1–6; 3:1–3).

Say: **While Jonah was still fish food, he talked with God and said, "I get it. I need to obey you. Give me another chance and I'm your guy."** That's when God had the fish vomit him onto a beach (whip off the blanket), **and Jonah lost no time telling the Wicked People about God. And getting a bath. Maybe not in that order.**

Ask kids to discuss:

- **Why do you think God gave Jonah a second chance instead of just sending someone else?**
- **What's a time in your life when you needed forgiveness?**

Before kids answer, form them into groups of no more than four.

Then tell an age-appropriate story about a time you needed someone's forgiveness—and got it. Model the sort of story you're hoping to hear, and be ready to deal with a delay before a child chooses to share a story after you finish talking.

That long silence is your kids deciding whether it's safe to share aloud. Your patience and silent encouragement will help them decide that it is.

Allow plenty of time for stories—this discussion is the heart of this session.

When kids have finished speaking, say: **Anyone who thinks he doesn't need a second chance is kidding himself.**

Read aloud Romans 3:23.

Say: **We've all sinned. We've all done wrong things. We all need God's forgiveness and grace. And there's good news: God gives second chances!**

CLOSING PRAYER

STEP AWAY, STEP BACK PRAYER
Time: about 5 minutes
Supplies: none

Ask kids to form a circle in the middle of the room and to hold hands.

Say: **If you've ever told a lie, let go of the hands you're holding.** (pause)

If you've ever been selfish, take a step back. (pause)

If you've ever hurt somebody's feelings, turn around and face away from the circle. (pause)

If you've ever taken something that's not yours—even for a little while—take another step away from the center of the circle behind you. (pause)

Pause and briefly confess aloud that you're all in need of a second chance. And not just the kids, but you too.

Then say: **If you've ever been sorry for something you've done, turn around and face the center of the circle again.** (pause)

If you've ever forgiven someone else for doing something that hurt you, take a step forward. (pause)

If you've asked someone to forgive you, take another step. (pause)

If you've asked God to forgive you, take the hands of the people next to you. (pause)

Pause and lead the kids in thanking God for his forgiveness—and for second chances.

EXTRA-TIME ACTIVITY—OPTION 1

20 CHANCES
Time: about 10 minutes
Supplies: none

Ask kids to each think of an object—an object that's more general than specific. For instance, "a goldfish" rather than "my pet goldfish, Sunny."

After one child volunteers to go first, help the rest of the kids ask yes and no questions so they can identify the object in 20 questions or fewer.

After playing several rounds, say: **You got a lot of second chances in this game!**

Ask kids to discuss:

- **How many second chances do you give someone who hurts you, before you give up on that person?**
- **Do you think there's a limit as to how many second chances God gives us? Why do you answer as you do?**

EXTRA-TIME ACTIVITY—OPTION 2

SECOND-CHANCE SKETCHES

Time: about 5 minutes
Supplies: 2 sheets of paper and a pencil per child, stopwatch

Say: **Congratulations! You're now all officially Upside-Down Artists!**

Your job is to draw a sketch of me ... but to draw me upside down. I'll pose and you'll have up to two minutes to sketch me with my head at the bottom of your sheet of paper and my toes at the top.

I'm so excited to launch my modeling career, so please start now!

Strike a dramatic pose, and after two minutes have kids compare sketches. Then have them use their second sheets of paper to try drawing you right-side up.

After two minutes have kids compare sketches. Applaud all work, declaring it front-of-refrigerator worthy.

Say: **I love the first sketches, but can I tell you a secret? I'm glad I gave you a second chance!**

EXTRA-TIME ACTIVITY—OPTION 3

NONSTOP 60

Time: about 5 minutes
Supplies: hat, index cards, pen, stopwatch

Before kids arrive, write a different topic on each index card. For instance:

- Your favorite insect
- Why you like or dislike cats

- Why chocolate ice cream is better than vanilla ice cream
- What to do if you're chased by a tiger

Place the cards in a hat.

Say: **God gave Jonah a second chance to talk with the people of Nineveh. But I'm giving you just one chance to talk nonstop for 60 seconds about … well, whatever you draw out of this hat.**

Explain that kids must talk for 60 seconds without hesitating, repeating themselves, or drifting off topic. Say: **It's harder than it sounds, but let's give it a try!**

Ask for a volunteer to go first and draw a card out of the hat. After a five-second pause, start the countdown—and the talking!

After kids have taken turns talking, ask:

- **If you had just 60 seconds to tell why it's good that God gives us second chances, what would you say?**

How God Used
a Fish with a Coin

The Point: God wants us to do the right thing.
Scripture Connect: Matthew 17:24–27

Supplies for all session 7 activities and options: stopwatch, nickels, duct tape, bowl, Bible, clean socks (a *lot* of them!), dollar bills (1 per child)

The Basics for Leaders

Back in Jesus's day, if you were a Jewish man at least 20 years old, you were expected to pay an annual temple tax. The money was used to keep the temple in good repair and temple activities humming along.

Nobody came to arrest you if you failed to pay the money. But paying the tax was considered the right thing to do, so people did it.

Doing the "right thing" is tricky. Not everyone agrees what the right thing is, and not everyone steps up to do it.

Today you'll help your kids explore how to do the right thing when it really *does* matter—when that right thing is something God expects them to do.

OPENING ACTIVITY-OPTION 1

TELL ME THUMBTHING
Time: about 5 minutes, depending on attendance
Supplies: none

After kids arrive, say: **When people like a movie, they sometimes give it a thumbs-up.** Demonstrate. **Really like the movie? Two thumbs-up. If they** dislike or really dislike the movie, they give it one or two thumbs-down. Demonstrate.

Please rate how this past week has gone for you. Was it a one or two thumbs-up week? A one or two thumbs-down week? Or maybe you'd give it one thumbs-up and one thumbs-down—it was a good *and* bad week.

Rate your week now.

After kids rate their weeks, give kids 30 seconds each to explain why they rated their weeks as they did. You'll go first, sharing a story that models the sort of brief, personal stories you hope kids will share too.

Children will express themselves more over time, and hearing their stories will help you adapt this session to make it even more relevant to your kids' lives.

OPENING ACTIVITY–OPTION 2

IT'S THE RIGHT THING SHAPE-UP

Time: about 5 minutes
Supplies: stopwatch

Ask kids to stand close together in an open area of the room.

Explain that you'll call out a shape and kids will have 45 seconds (adjust as you see fit) to use their bodies to create that shape. Extra credit if they can make it a three-dimensional version.

> **AGE-ALERT TIPS**
> Pair **older kids** with **younger kids**. And if a pair finishes early, have them help another pair who may be struggling.

Say: **Two things—first, you can talk to one another but not to me. And second, making shapes is the right thing to do because, if you don't, aliens from the galaxy Zookbot will turn us all into asparagus spears. So … get ready!**

Call out these shapes or substitute others: square, oval, car, can of soup, rhombus. Add urgency by counting down the time.

When kids finish, talk about this:

- **What made this easy or hard?**
- **If you could have asked me a question, what would it have been?**

Thank kids for sharing their answers, and then say: **Doing the right thing is hard when you're not sure exactly what the right thing is. Or when it makes you uncomfortable or costs you something.**

We'll talk more about that, but first a game of Note the Nickels!

Amazing Animals Game

NOTE THE NICKELS

Time: about 10 minutes

Supplies: 20 nickels, duct tape, bowl, stopwatch

Before children arrive, hide 19 nickels in the room. Then duct-tape one nickel to the bottom of your shoe. Be careful that kids don't see the bottom of your shoe!

Place a bowl on the floor in the middle of your room.

Say: **If you were hiding coins in this room, where would you conceal them?**

Ask kids to call out their suggestions, and then explain: **20 nickels are hidden, and you have two minutes to find them and drop them into the bowl, starting ... now!**

When two minutes have passed, gather kids together and count the nickels in the bowl. Reveal other hiding spots—except the nickel on the bottom of your shoe.

As a group talk about:

- **Tell about a time you found or lost money. What happened, and how did it feel?**
- **If you found a million dollars and could keep it, what would you do with it?**
- **If someone told you to go to the grocery store and crack open an egg so you could find a silver coin, would you do it? Why or why not?**

Remove the nickel on the bottom of your shoe and toss it into the bowl.

Say: **Let's hear about a time someone found a coin in a really, really strange place. He found it because he was helping Jesus do the right thing!**

Amazing Animals Bible Story

FISH FACE

Time: about 20 minutes
Supplies: Bible

Say: **Welcome to the dress rehearsal of the new play Fish Face. And you're the actors!**

Cast kids in these roles: Jesus, Peter, the tax gatherers, and the fish. If you have lots of kids, add more fish. Just a few kids? Cut the tax gatherers and *you* play the fish.

Give your actors this background information: **Jesus is at a home in Capernaum, one probably owned by Peter. Men show up to collect the annual temple tax, money that every Jewish man 20 years old or older is expected to pay. The money helps take care of temple expenses in Jerusalem.**

It isn't exactly a law that you have to pay, but paying is considered the right thing to do.

Let's pick up the story from there.

Read aloud Matthew 17:24–27, pausing so actors can fill in the action. Encourage the fish to keep making fish faces.

When the production ends, applaud wildly. Then sit with kids to discuss:

- **Why do you think Jesus asked if kings taxed their own people or people they'd conquered?**
- **Jesus wanted to do the right thing even if he wasn't required to pay the tax. When did you do something just because it was the right thing to do?**
- **If you could change one "right thing" people expect you to do, what would it be?**

Say: **You don't always do the right thing. I know that because I don't always do the right thing either—and we're a lot alike. We all make mistakes. But sometimes when we don't do the right thing, it's not a mistake. We just decide to do what's wrong.**

Here's the good news: God will forgive us if we come to him and honestly ask for forgiveness. So let's do that now.

CLOSING PRAYER

CLOSING PRAYER

COURAGE PRAYER

Time: about 5 minutes
Supplies: none

Ask kids to sit in a circle on the floor and close their eyes.

Explain that you'll mention something for them to do and then something to silently pray about as you pause. Pauses will last about 20 seconds each.

Say: **Please touch your lips.** (pause as kids do as you asked) Pray: **God, please help us to do the right thing with our words. Sometimes we say mean things or lie.**

If you've said hurtful words or told a lie, silently tell God what it was and ask for his forgiveness. (pause for 20 seconds)

Please touch your closed eyes. (pause as kids do as you asked)

God, sometimes we look at things that we shouldn't see. Online, on television, at the movies—we see pictures and videos that don't honor you or others.

If you've done that, silently tell God about it and ask for his forgiveness. (pause for 20 seconds)

Please touch your ears. (pause as kids do as you asked)

God, sometimes we listen when we shouldn't. When someone is spreading stories or rumors, we listen even when we know we should walk away.

If you've done that, silently tell God what happened and ask for his forgiveness. (pause for 20 seconds)

Please touch your feet. (pause as kids do as you asked)

God, sometimes we go where we shouldn't go.

If you've done that, silently tell God about it and ask for his forgiveness. (pause for 20 seconds)

And now please put your hands together (pause as kids do as you asked)

God, sometimes we do things that don't please you. Forgive us—and give us a heart for you. Give us a deep desire to not just avoid doing what's wrong. Help us love doing what's right—what pleases you.

Amen.

Ask kids to talk about this:

- **Tell about a time you asked for forgiveness for something you did to someone and you were forgiven. How did you** feel before you were forgiven? How did you feel after you were forgiven?

Say: **The truth is you won't always do the right thing. That's because—hard to believe but true—you're not perfect. So I'm glad God is always ready to forgive us.**

Let's be quick to forgive one another too!

EXTRA-TIME ACTIVITY—OPTION 1

CALL IT!

Time: about 5 minutes
Supplies: nickels, stopwatch

Ask kids to form pairs and for each pair to decide who's the flipper and who's the caller. Give the flipper in each pair a nickel.

Explain that as flippers flip or toss their nickels into the air, the callers are to call out either "heads" or "tails." The goal is for a pair to correctly predict the outcome three times in a row.

When a pair is successful, have that pair shout out, "We called it!"

Some pairs will get lucky and predict three flips correctly, and others won't—so put a two-minute time limit on this game. Encourage winning pairs to keep playing. Maybe they'll get lucky twice!

When time has elapsed, gather up the nickels and ask kids to discuss:

- Was this a game of luck, skill, or both? Why?
- What—if anything—could you do to increase your chances of winning?
- The right thing to do was to call out the right outcome three times in a row—but you couldn't make that happen. Tell about a time you knew what was the right thing to do, but you just couldn't do it.

EXTRA-TIME ACTIVITY—OPTION 2

INSTANT FEEDBACK

Time: about 10 minutes
Supplies: clean socks (a lot of them!)

Before kids arrive, ball up a bunch of clean socks.

Give each child three socks and explain that you'll all juggle three socks—starting with just one sock. Quickly check to see if you've got a juggler in the crowd. If so, ask for a demonstration.

Say: **The right thing to do with juggling is to keep everything you're juggling in the air. Simple, right? How hard can it be?**

Let's see how it goes.

At your signal, ask kids to add a second and then third sock. If socks fall, it's okay to start again. Practice makes perfect … or not!

Say: **It wasn't hard for Peter to catch a fish—he was a fisherman! But he found it hard to always control his temper and his tongue.**

Discuss:

- **What's something you struggle to control as you try to do the right thing?**

Wrap up by asking Jesus for help.

EXTRA-TIME ACTIVITY–OPTION 3

DO-RIGHT DOLLARS

Time: about 5 minutes
Supplies: dollar bills (1 per child)

Give each child a dollar bill and then ask:

- **What might you do to serve another person with a dollar?**

Challenge kids to ask Jesus to help them serve with the dollar. Say you'll ask them to report back what happened the next time you all get together (and make a note to do that!).

Say: **Ask Jesus to guide you to do the right thing.**

How God Used
Sheep

The Point: God loves us.
Scripture Connect: Luke 15:3–7

Supplies for all session 8 activities and options: aluminum foil (cut sheets 18" long, 3 per child), clear tape, safety scissors, stopwatch, smartphone, string, Bible, large paper clips (or chenille wire, 1 per child)

The Basics for Leaders

Some Jewish religious leaders had a problem with Jesus: he was hanging out with questionable people. People no self-respecting rabbi should talk to, let alone share a meal with.

Tax collectors. Sinners. Prostitutes.

But Jesus didn't apologize. Instead, he shared a story about a lost sheep and faithful shepherd, which revealed his heart for those who need him most. And it's a heart brimming with love.

In this session you'll help your kids know—and trust—that Jesus loves them. You'll help them not just hear the words, but discover the truth: They're loved. Profoundly, deeply, sincerely, utterly to-the-ends-of-the-earth loved.

And you know what? You're loved too.

OPENING ACTIVITY–OPTION 1

TELL ME THUMBTHING
Time: about 5 minutes, depending on attendance
Supplies: none

After kids arrive, say: **When people like a movie, they sometimes give it a thumbs-up.** Demonstrate. **Really like the movie? Two thumbs-up. If they dislike or really dislike the movie, they give it one or two thumbs-down.** Demonstrate.

Please rate how this past week has gone for you. Was it a one or two thumbs-up week? A one or two thumbs-down week? Or maybe you'd give it one thumbs-up and one thumbs-down—it was a good *and* bad week.

Rate your week now.

After kids rate their weeks, give kids 30 seconds each to explain why they rated their weeks as they did. You'll go first, sharing a story that models the sort of brief, personal stories you hope kids will share too.

Children will express themselves more over time, and hearing their stories will help you adapt this session to make it even more relevant to your kids' lives.

OPENING ACTIVITY—OPTION 2

WHO'S THERE?

Time: about 10 minutes
Supplies: aluminum foil (cut sheets 18" long, 3 per child), clear tape, safety scissors, stopwatch, smartphone

Place supplies where they can be easily accessed by kids. Explain that you'd like them to create masks using just foil and tape.

Say: **Usually people wear masks that hide who they are. But not us! We'll make masks that reveal something about who we are.**

For instance, if you really like dogs, you might make a dog face mask. Love soccer? Make a soccer ball mask. It's up to you, but you'll only have five minutes to make your mask.

You'll hold it up to your face, so be sure to make eye holes so you can see.

Ready? Start now!

Encourage kids as they work. If a child can't think about what to make, help by asking questions until the child shares a favorite thing that's mask-worthy.

When kids have finished or time has passed, ask kids to show their masks and explain what the masks reveal about themselves.

Then use a phone to take a picture of each child. Later, forward the picture to the kids' phones or their parents' phones with a note about what the mask reveals.

Ask kids to discuss:

- **When you meet people, what's something you want them to know about you? What's something you don't want them to know?**
- **Tell about a time you got to know someone better and found that you liked them more.**
- **Tell about a time you got to know someone better and found that you didn't like the person as much.**

Thank kids for sharing their stories.

Say: **I have some good news for you! Jesus knows you. He knows all about you—what you do, say, and even think. Nobody knows you better.**

Jesus knows you're not perfect. But he still loves you. He loves you right now, just as you are. He wants a friendship with you that lasts forever, a friendship that will change everything for you.

That's not just good news—it's great news!

In a few minutes, we'll talk about a story Jesus shared about someone who did a really good job of knowing and loving others.

But first, a quick game of Scooting Shepherd!

Amazing Animals Game

SCOOTING SHEPHERD
Time: about 10 minutes
Supplies: string

Define the boundaries of your "pasture" playing area by laying string on the floor.

Ask for a volunteer—that person will be the shepherd. The rest of the kids will be sheep.

Explain that the sheep have to be on all fours and can go anywhere in the pasture. The shepherd can go anywhere too but has to scoot on his or her bottom to get there. The goal of the game is for the shepherd to tag sheep who, once touched, become shepherds themselves and join in trying to touch sheep.

Say: **Shepherd, you've got a problem. All your sheep are running loose. That means they can fall off cliffs or get eaten by wolves. You have to go get them so you can keep them safe ... starting now!**

After all the sheep have been turned into shepherds, play again—this time with the sheep having to scoot too.

After the game has ended, say: **A good shepherd does whatever it takes to care for his or her sheep. In all sorts of weather, day or night, the shepherd is there, ready to help.**

As a group discuss:

- **Who in your life is like that shepherd? Always ready to help, no matter what?**
- **Why do you think that person cares so much?**
- **Who in your life is so important to you that you'd do any-thing to help the person?**

Say: **There's someone who loves you so much that he'd do whatever it takes to help you—and that's Jesus. And he not only loves you, he also likes you.**

Let's hear how Jesus explained his love in a story he told about a shepherd and an especially high-maintenance sheep.

Amazing Animals **Bible Story**

HIDE-AND-SEEK SHEEP

Time: about 15 minutes
Supplies: stopwatch, Bible

Ask one older, trustworthy child to go hide somewhere close by as if you're playing a game of hide-and-seek. If you're in a large building, set limits about where the child can hide!

Give the child a two-minute head start while you explain to the rest of the kids that you'll be searching for the lost sheep who's wandered off. But be clear: you'll be searching as one group; everyone has to stay close together. To help that happen, have kids link elbows and form a clump—and you join in too.

Keep one arm free so you can hold a Bible and read aloud as you search. Read Luke 15:3-4 as you lead the search for your missing sheep.

Once you find the child who's hiding, read aloud Luke 15:5-7, unlink elbows, and join in loud applause and cheering—what was lost has been found! It's time to celebrate!

Have kids sit together, and then say: **Jesus was talking to people who knew a lot about sheep and shepherds. They knew that sheep can't take care of themselves out in the world and need help just living through the day. Without the help and protection of a shepherd—a good one—sheep don't last long.**

As a group discuss:

- **Jesus is saying he's a shepherd—a good one. In what ways do you think that's true?**
- **In what ways have you seen Jesus love you this past week— or have you not seen that?**
- **In this story we're the sheep. In what ways do you think we're like sheep?**

Say: **I don't always like thinking of myself as a sheep. I want to believe I'm powerful and can take care of myself, but that's not true. Not always.**

I really do need a shepherd—someone who cares for me. Who helps me. Who comes looking for me when I wander off into bad stuff.

That's one reason I not only need Jesus as my shepherd, but I want him as my shepherd. I say yes when he asks me to follow him.

Because I know he loves me, it's easy for me to decide to follow him. Let's talk with him about that now.

CLOSING PRAYER

WILLING SHEEP PRAYER

Time: about 5 minutes
Supplies: none

Ask kids to sit in a circle.

Explain that you'll lead a prayer in which everyone gets to call out words that add to the prayer. For instance, you might say "God, here's how we feel about you," and kids might say "love" or "awesome" or "happy."

Pray: **God, thank you for loving us. When we think about how much you love us, we feel …** (pause as kids add words)

Jesus is such a great shepherd. We thank him for what he's done for us. Things like … (pause as kids add words)

We want to be sheep who don't wander off, but sometimes that's what we do. Sometimes we wander off and do things like … (pause as kids add words)

But when we ask, you forgive us, God. Thank you. Thank you that your love is higher and wider and deeper than our mistakes. Thank you that your love is now and forever.

Amen.

EXTRA-TIME ACTIVITY—OPTION 1

ALL TOGETHER NOW

Time: about 5 minutes
Supplies: stopwatch

Ask kids to form pairs, and give each pair the same assignment: find five things you have in common.

For instance, maybe both kids have three people in their families. Or are in the same grade at school. Or like the same baseball team. Or both have names that have six letters.

When kids find five things they have in common, have them give each other a high five. Ten things: a high 10. Twenty things? Well, both feet and hands have to get involved.

Allow up to three minutes for pairs to work, and then ask the entire group to call out some of the things they found they have in common.

When kids have finished, say: **Here's the thing that I think is most important that we all have in common—God loves us! And that's something to really celebrate!**

Have kids all stand and see if everyone in the room can exchange a high five in fewer than 10 seconds.

EXTRA-TIME ACTIVITY–OPTION 2

HEART CHAIN

Time: about 5 minutes
Supplies: large paper clips (or chenille wire, 1 per child)

This is about the simplest craft possible, but that's fine; the idea is to give your kids something to do with their hands as they talk together as a group.

Explain that you want a chain of hearts to hang in the room, a reminder that you're all loved by Jesus. Ask that each child create a heart by bending a paper clip into a heart shape.

Ask kids to discuss these questions as they work:

> **AGE-ALERT TIPS**
> If you have **younger children**, substitute chenille wire for paper clips; it's easier to bend and there's less chance of an accidental stabbing.

- Sometimes being loving means being tough or honest with someone. What's something Jesus said or did that was loving—but tough?
- What's something tough that Jesus said in the Bible that sounds like he means those words for you?
- God loves us. What's that say about us ... and what's it say about God?

String kids' hearts together and loop the chain over a chair or curtain rod so it's visible in the room as a reminder: you're all loved by God.

EXTRA-TIME ACTIVITY–OPTION 3

SHOW-AND-TELL

Time: about 10 minutes
Supplies: none

Say: **God's love isn't something given to us to keep to ourselves. It's something we share!** Ask:

- **How can you show God's love? What can you do?**
- **How can you tell others about God's love? What can you say?**

Wrap up your discussion with a quick prayer for opportunities to show God's love and talk about it. And for the courage to take advantage of such opportunities.

How God Used
a Young Donkey

The Point: God wants us to know Jesus is King.
Scripture Connect: Mark 11:1–10

Supplies for all session 9 activities and options: 30 balloons, 2 trash bags, 2 XXL button-up shirts (or sweaters), stopwatch, 1 pin, Bibles, paper, safety scissors, markers, clear tape, Cheerios cereal, resealable plastic snack bags, duct tape, paper towels, water

The Basics for Leaders

The people Jesus met were looking for a king. God had promised to send one. They needed one. So they were always scanning the horizon, awaiting a king's arrival.

They just didn't expect their king to look like Jesus.

Where was his army? His crown? Why wasn't he leading them into battle, pushing the Romans out of Israel?

Jesus might be an interesting teacher, sure, but a King?

The people who dismissed Jesus got it wrong. They missed seeing him for who he truly was and still is.

Yes, Jesus *is* a teacher. He *is* the Savior. He *is* the Son of God. But he's also the King–the *King* of Kings.

In this session your kids will not only discover that Jesus is a King but that he's *their* King.

OPENING ACTIVITY—OPTION 1

TELL ME THUMBTHING

Time: about 5 minutes, depending on attendance
Supplies: none

After kids arrive, say: **When people like a movie, they sometimes give it a thumbs-up.** Demonstrate. **Really like the movie? Two thumbs-up. If they dislike or really dislike the movie, they give it one or two thumbs-down.** Demonstrate.

Please rate how this past week has gone for you. Was it a one or two thumbs-up week? A one or two thumbs-down week? Or maybe you'd give it one thumbs-up and one thumbs-down—it was a good *and* bad week.

Rate your week now.

After kids rate their weeks, give kids 30 seconds each to explain why they rated their weeks as they did. You'll go first, sharing a story that models the sort of brief, personal stories you hope kids will share too.

Children will express themselves more over time, and hearing their stories will help you adapt this session to make it even more relevant to your kids' lives.

OPENING ACTIVITY—OPTION 2

FIRST IN LINE

Time: about 10 minutes
Supplies: none

Ask kids to line up, side by side, against a wall.

Explain that they've all been drafted into the Royal Balloon Stuffing Corps (RBSC) and you're the official RBSC assistant training coach. It's your job to get them shaped up and in order before reporting to duty.

Ask kids to line up—from your left to your right—by height, tallest to smallest.

Encourage them to line up quickly; their Royal Balloon Stuffing Corps training will begin in just minutes.

Then have kids line up in other ways. Each time, switch whether they line up left to right, right to left, back to front, or front to back. Some lineup options: alphabetically, by middle name, by birthday, by who's wearing the most blue, by longest hair, by most money in their pocket, by number of pets, by number of letters in their last name.

Keep the activity moving swiftly—it's okay if there's some confusion and the lineup isn't absolutely accurate.

Finally, ask kids to line up front to back by who's most important. *That* will be a stopper.

Ask kids to sit in a circle and talk about this:

- **How did you feel when I asked you to line up by who's most important? Why?**
- **Tell about a time that you felt important—really important. What was the situation?**

Say: **That last lineup was a hard one—because we like to think that everyone's important. And everyone is! But if there had been a king in the room, we probably would've pushed him to the front of the line.**

Today we'll meet a King. But first, Royal Balloon Stuffing Corps cadets, it's time for you to show what you can do!

Amazing Animals Game

BALLOON STUFFING

Time: 5 minutes
Supplies: 30 balloons, 2 trash bags, 2 XXL button-up shirts (or sweaters), stopwatch, 1 pin

Before kids arrive, inflate the balloons and place 15 in each of the trash bags. Hide the bags.

You'll ask for two volunteers, but do that *after* you describe this game. You want volunteers who are wearing pants and who know what they'll be doing.

Give each of your volunteers a shirt. Have your volunteers tuck the bottom of the large shirts into their pants but leave the top few buttons of the shirts unbuttoned.

Form the rest of your kids into two teams—one around each volunteer.

Explain: You've blown up two garbage bags full of balloons. The job of the teams is to stuff the balloons inside the large shirt of your volunteer. Say: **The goal is to stuff more balloons inside your shirt than the other team can stuff into their shirt.**

Teams will have one minute to insert balloons when you give the signal. If they want to keep going at one minute, add an additional round of 30 seconds.

Expect chaos!

When kids have finished, count the number of balloons each team has left over. Whichever team has fewest—they're the winner. Another way to tell is to use a pin to burst the balloons through the shirts of your volunteers and to have the group count aloud the number of pops. If you choose this option for counting, be careful—and sensitive to the location of body parts.

Thank your volunteers and say this to the winning team: **It's fun to be a winner, but do keep in mind this isn't an Olympic sport. There are no balloon-stuffing college scholarships ... at least not yet.**

Say: **Sometimes people describe very important people as "puffed up"—they think they're better than they really are. They have more power than everyone else. They're on the covers of magazines. Everyone knows who they are.**

Not every important person is like that ... but some are.

The one we'll meet today was a king—but he wasn't puffed up. In fact, most people didn't even know he was a king.

Especially when he rode into town on a donkey.

Amazing Animals **Bible Story**

BIBLE BRAY

Time: about 20 minutes
Supplies: Bible

Explain that you'll read aloud a passage from the Bible, but need help with sound effects.

Tell kids they'll all play the part of a donkey, which means they'll be braying, making the sound donkeys make. Ask them to do that several times, and afterwards point out that a donkey bray is described differently in various languages. Assign these different versions of braying to one or more kids:

- Icelandic: E-Haw Haw
- Hebrew: Yi-Ah
- Turkish A-Iiii A-Iiii
- French: Hihan
- Dutch: I-A

After kids practice their donkey brays, tell kids to shout out every time they hear you say *donkey*. Then read aloud Mark 11:1–10.

Take some liberties: be sure to work the word *donkey* in often by adding details that aren't necessarily in the text. For example, "The donkey (bray) was a nice donkey (bray) who had a lot of donkey (bray) friends."

When you've finished reading, have kids let out with a couple of full-volume brays to wrap up, and then, as a group, discuss:

- **In what ways did people show Jesus they thought he was their King?**

When you ask the next question, lead by sharing your answer to the question.

- **In what ways do you show Jesus you think he's your King? And how might you do that more?**

Say: **Many years before Jesus showed up on a donkey, the prophet Zechariah described how Israel's king would come into Jerusalem.**

Read aloud Zechariah 9:9–10.

Say: **You can see why people were excited that Jesus came into Jerusalem riding on a donkey. And why they thought Jesus would get rid of the Romans and make Israel a great nation again.**

But Jesus didn't come to just set up a new kingdom in Israel and be king of the Jews. He came to set up a kingdom that would last forever, and to be the King of everything—including our hearts.

God wants us to know that Jesus is *the* King … our King!

CLOSING PRAYER

THREE-MINUTE CROWNS

Time: about 5 minutes
Supplies: paper, safety scissors, markers, clear tape, Bible, stopwatch

Place the art supplies where kids can easily access them.

Explain: Kids will have three minutes to create crowns—crowns they'll wear. Tell kids to use markers to add as much bling as possible to their crowns because that's what kings and queens do.

Join in creating a crown, and place the Bible nearby as kids work.

After three minutes (adjust the time if you'd like), put on your crown and have kids put on their crowns.

Say: **I've got some good news for you and some not-so-good news.**

First the not-so-good news: we're not really kings and queens. Even if we sometimes act that way, it's not true.

But we do know a King—a real one.

Take off your crown and place it by the Bible.

Say: **Jesus is my King. If you want to let Jesus know he's your King too, come place your crown by the Bible.**

After kids do—or don't—place their crowns by the Bible, ask them to join you in thanking Jesus for being your King.

EXTRA-TIME ACTIVITY—OPTION 1

20 CHANCES

Time: about 5 minutes
Supplies: Cheerios cereal

Ask kids to form pairs, and have one partner in each pair lie flat on the ground, facing up.

The goal of this game is for the vertical partners to stack as many Cheerios as possible on the noses of their horizontal partners.

Declare the owner of the tallest tower of minicrowns the Emperor of Cheerios.

Wrap up by passing the box of cereal around and allowing some snacking!

EXTRA-TIME ACTIVITY—OPTION 2

SEEING JESUS CLEARLY

Time: about 10 minutes
Supplies: resealable plastic snack bags, duct tape, paper towels, Bibles, water

You'll help kids create magnifying glasses and focus on how Jesus is King!

Have kids fill their resealable bags with water, and then securely seal the bags. If you're worried about spillage, add duct tape over the seals.

Use paper towels to wipe the outside of the bags completely dry. Then place the bags over open pages of the Bible. Kids will discover that the print will be magnified.

Have kids look up these passages and read them out loud: John 18:37; Revelation 17:14; 1 Timothy 6:15–16; Isaiah 9:6.

Ask kids to discuss:

- **After reading these verses, what words would you use to describe King Jesus?**

EXTRA-TIME ACTIVITY—OPTION 3

WELCOME, KING! MINI-POSTERS

Time: about 10 minutes
Supplies: paper, markers

Explain that you'll be joining the crowds lining the streets in Jerusalem as Jesus comes by on a donkey. But instead of tossing your coats on the ground, you'll be holding up signs.

Ask kids to each design a sign they'll hold up.

After kids finish, have them show their signs and discuss:

AGE-ALERT TIPS

If you have **younger kids** who can't write words, have them draw something—whatever they'd like.

- **Why did you choose what you put on your sign?**
- **What do you think Jesus would say if he saw your sign?**

Say: **Jesus does see our signs—because he's here with us. Let's all hold up our signs and give King Jesus a big cheer!**

How God Used
a School of Fish

The Point: God wants us to obey him.
Scripture Connect: Luke 5:1–11

Supplies for all session 10 activities and options: 8' lengths of clothesline rope (1 per every 2 kids), scissors, Bible, cardboard box, opened bag of Twizzler style rope candy, pillow, stopwatch

The Basics for Leaders

Obey probably isn't your kids' favorite word. You might not be fond of it either.

But in the kingdom of God, obedience is more than just doing what you've been told to do. It's a sign of trust, a way of letting God know we love him.

Obedience also carries us out of our independence and deeper into a friendship with God. It lifts us onto safe ground, shaping and molding us into the image of our Creator.

In this session you'll help kids discover that *obey* isn't a dirty word. Rather, it's a word that ultimately sets them free.

OPENING ACTIVITY–OPTION 1

TELL ME THUMBTHING

Time: about 5 minutes, depending on attendance
Supplies: none

After kids arrive, say: **When people like a movie, they sometimes give it a thumbs-up.** Demonstrate. **Really like the movie? Two thumbs-up. If they** dislike or really dislike the movie, they give it one or two thumbs-down. Demonstrate.

Please rate how this past week has gone for you. Was it a one or two thumbs-up week? A one or two thumbs-down week? Or maybe you'd give it one thumbs-up and one thumbs-down—it was a good *and* bad week.

Rate your week now.

After kids rate their weeks, give kids 30 seconds each to explain why they rated their weeks as they did. You'll go first, sharing a story that models the sort of brief, personal stories you hope kids will share too.

Children will express themselves more over time, and hearing their stories will help you adapt this session to make it even more relevant to your kids' lives.

OPENING ACTIVITY—OPTION 2

HARDER THAN IT LOOKS

Time: about 10 minutes
Supplies: 8' lengths of clothesline rope (1 per every 2 kids), scissors

Before kids arrive cut the lengths of rope.

Ask kids to stand in a circle, and as you speak, tangle the lengths of rope. You want the pieces to be snarled, but not so tangled that there are tight knots.

Step into the circle and hold the tangle of rope at the height of kids' waists.

Instruct kids to each take a step forward, grab the end of a piece of rope, and tie it around a belt loop. If a child doesn't have belt loops, you can tie it around his or her wrist.

Each child will now be tied to another—but they won't know who. If you have an even number of kids, you're set—just be sure to include one piece of rope for every two kids in your circle. If there's an odd number of kids, you'll join in yourself.

Say: **What I want you to do is untangle these ropes without untying the ropes from your belt loops. Good luck!**

When kids have finished, have them untie the ropes from their belt loops and sit down. As a group discuss:

• **What made it easy or hard to obey my request?**

- Tell about a time that obeying what someone told you to do was harder than it first seemed.
- What's something Jesus expects you to do that you're not sure you can do?

Say: **Obeying others can be hard—really hard. Let's talk more about that right after a quick game of Crab Walk!**

Amazing Animals Game

CRAB WALK
Time: about 5 minutes
Supplies: none

Ask kids to sit on the floor in a line facing you.

Explain that you'll be talking about how a school of fish made a surprise appearance. You'll ask kids to pretend they are fish, but there's no water. So instead, they're crabs. Crabs who'll walk in formation.

Have kids assume the "crab walk" position: stomachs aimed toward the ceiling, feet and hands flat on the floor, bottoms lifted into the air. If a child—or you—can't hold the position, it's okay to scoot on one's bottom.

Tell kids you'll give them instructions about which direction to move—forward, backward, to their left, or to their right. The goal is for them to obey every instruction immediately so they can avoid crab collisions.

Run kids through switching directions at least 10 times, at an increasingly fast pace, until your crabs collapse.

Then sit together on the floor and discuss:

- That was a tough workout! When it comes to obeying orders, would you rather be giving orders or taking them? Why?
- When is it hardest to obey? When is it easiest?
- What's an order you'd love to give and have everyone obey.

Say: **Earlier I mentioned some fish obeying an order. Let's join them now and see how things turn out for them—and for the guys who caught them.**

Amazing Animals Bible Story

FISHY STORY

Time: about 15 minutes
Supplies: Bible

Tell kids they'll act out an event described in the Bible. Assign these roles: Jesus, Peter, James, John, and the fish. Anyone who doesn't have a role as a person will play as part of the group of fish.

Before launching into the story, say: **There are a couple things you should know.**

First, Simon Peter (we'll call him Peter), James, and John are professional fishermen, so they're experts when it comes to using nets to catch fish. Also, fishermen back in Jesus's day always fished at night—otherwise fish would see the nets and just avoid getting caught.

And then there's this: sometimes even really great fishermen don't catch anything. Sad, but true.

Position your fish off to one side of the room and your people in the center of the room. Say: **Lights! Camera! Action!** Then read aloud Luke 5:1–11.

Pause throughout so actors can do what you're describing. And have fun with this—add details along the way that give your actors more direction. For instance, "'Master,' Peter replied, sighing and rolling his eyes, 'we worked hard all last night …'"

When you've finished acting out this passage, applaud wildly. Then have kids sit and, as a group, discuss:

- **What did you discover about Jesus from this event? About Peter? About James and John? About fish?**
- **Who in this story obeyed? Was their obedience a good thing or not?**
- **Peter, James, and John left everything and followed Jesus. Do you think he asks you to do that too? Why?**

Say: **Sorry, fish. Obeying Jesus means you got served up for dinner. But everyone else who obeyed was blessed and found a new purpose in life.**

When Jesus asks us to obey him, it's always for a reason—and always for our good!

CLOSING PRAYER

OBEDIENCE PRAYER

Time: about 5 minutes
Supplies: cardboard box, opened bag of Twizzler style rope candy

Have the bag of candy hidden inside the closed cardboard box. Ask kids to sit in a circle.

Say: **Most of us aren't fans of the word** *obey.*

Usually that word means we're being told to do something we'd rather not do. So when we hear someone say "I want you to obey me," we don't like hearing it.

Even if it's God who's telling us to obey.

Explain that you're all going to pray for hearts that are willing and able to obey God. Not because God is bigger than us, or stronger than us, but because obeying God is the right thing to do … and the smart thing to do.

Place the cardboard box in the middle of your circle.

Say: **I know what's in this box—but you don't. It could be a bag of candy or a box with sleeping baby snakes.**

Please close your eyes and keep them closed until I tell you to open them. (pause as kids do as you've asked) **Now, with your eyes closed, each of you please hold one hand out in front of you, palm up.**

Open the box, making sure kids can hear you do so. Remind kids to keep their eyes closed, and ask them to hold their hands absolutely steady—no shaking or bending their fingers. Tell kids it's important that they obey you.

Continue speaking as you drape one piece of rope candy over each of their hands.

Say: **It comes down whether you trust me. Am I the sort of person who would give you candy or place a snake in your hand when you're not looking?**

When you've finished distributing candy, say: **Here's where you find out whether obeying me was smart … or stupid. Raise your hand and take a bite of what I put in your hand. Then open your eyes.**

As kids eat their candy, read aloud Psalm 34:8.

Say: **God is good—and when he tells us to do something, it's for our good. What God tells us to do may be hard and we may not understand it, but we can be sure of this: God is good. He loves us. And when we obey him, we're letting God know we trust and love him.**

Ask kids to again hold out a hand and close their eyes.

Pray: **God, give us the courage to trust you.**

Thank you that you know things we don't know. You know the future and what's waiting for each of us there. Thank you for walking with us through today and tomorrow and all our tomorrows.

We love you.

Amen.

EXTRA-TIME ACTIVITY–OPTION 1

FIRE DRILL

Time: about 10 minutes
Supplies: none

Tell kids that you're taking a safety break to practice evacuating the building should a fire alarm sound.

Show kids how to check to see if there's a fire on the other side of the door by feeling the door and doorknob for heat, and checking for smoke coming in through cracks around the door. No smoke? Then, with the back of your fingers, touch the doorknob. If it's cool and there's no smoke, open the door and immediately exit the building, staying low to the ground if you smell smoke.

Tell kids to take nothing with them—no pausing to gather up their stuff.

Practice exiting the building twice, showing kids where to gather a safe distance from the building.

After several practice rounds, ask kids to sit and discuss:

- **Why is it important that we obey the rules during a fire drill or an actual fire?**
- **In what ways do those same reasons apply to obeying what God tells us to do?**

EXTRA-TIME ACTIVITY–OPTION 2

KING OR QUEEN–FOR A MINUTE

Time: about 10 minutes
Supplies: pillow, stopwatch

Place the pillow on the floor and tell kids it's a throne. They should appreciate that because they'll take turns being king or queen—but only for a minute.

The goal: to give as many orders as possible in 60 seconds. The orders can be short (such as "Sit!" or "Be quiet!" or "Dance!") or they can be long (such as "Go draw me a bubble bath and make sure my rubber ducky is in it!"). But the orders have to come rapid-fire. Quantity matters!

Count down by calling out "Start" and "Stop" and by counting off the number of orders issued.

If you have more than five kids, consider making this a 30-second reign on the throne so the activity moves quicker. Give points for the number of orders called out and the creativity of the mandates.

When kids have had turns ruling, say: **I notice nobody was really serious about obeying the orders we heard. Let's talk about this.**

- **How do you decide who you have to obey and who you don't have to obey?**
- **When you think about God, how do those things you mentioned apply?**

EXTRA-TIME ACTIVITY—OPTION 3

FOLLOW THE LEADER-ISH

Time: about 5 minutes
Supplies: none

Ask kids to form a single-file line—you'll be last in line—and for the leader to walk around the room, making up actions as he or she goes. Raised arms, hops to the left or right, turning around to walk backward … it's all fair game.

Every 15 seconds or so call out "Switch," and the leader will rotate to the back of the line and a new leader will take charge.

Play until you rotate to the front of the line; then collapse to the floor and lie there. Kids will do the same. Sit up, form a circle, and talk about this:

- **How was that experience like or not like obeying God?**

How God Used
a Rooster

The Point: God is never surprised.
Scripture Connect: Luke 22:33–34, 54–62

Supplies for all session 11 activities and options: envelopes, marker, paper, pencils, Bible, 5 or 6 sticks

The Basics for Leaders

"Surprise!"

When it's a room full of friends shouting that word at a you-didn't-see-it-coming birthday party, it's one thing.

When the word sneaks into a medical diagnosis or comes at you in the form of a pop quiz, it's something else altogether.

Surprises can rock us back on our heels. Change everything instantly. Blow up our lives.

But God is *never* surprised—and he's willing to walk through all the surprises that interrupt our lives.

In this session you'll help your kids discover the peace of mind that comes with knowing the God who's often surprising—but never surprised.

OPENING ACTIVITY–OPTION 1

TELL ME THUMBTHING
Time: about 5 minutes, depending on attendance
Supplies: none

After kids arrive, say: **When people like a movie, they sometimes give it a thumbs-up.** Demonstrate. **Really like the movie? Two thumbs-up. If they dislike or really dislike the movie, they give it one or two thumbs-down.** Demonstrate.

Please rate how this past week has gone for you. Was it a one or two thumbs-up week? A one or two thumbs-down week? Or maybe you'd give it one thumbs-up and one thumbs-down—it was a good and **bad week. Rate your week now.**

After kids rate their weeks, give kids 30 seconds each to explain why they rated their weeks as they did. You'll go first, sharing a story that models the sort of brief, personal stories you hope kids will share too.

Children will express themselves more over time, and hearing their stories will help you adapt this session to make it even more relevant to your kids' lives.

OPENING ACTIVITY—OPTION 2

BEST-LAID PLANS

Time: about 5 minutes
Supplies: envelopes, marker, paper, pencils

Before class, label four envelopes—one "Place," one "Profession," one "Number," and one "Animal."

Distribute four slips of paper and a pencil to every person.

Ask kids (you do this too!) to write a number on a slip of paper. Collect those slips in the "Number" envelope.

AGE-ALERT TIPS
Younger children may need help filling out their slips of paper. Pair them with **older children**.

Do the same thing for the "Place," "Profession," and "Animal" envelopes—have kids write things for the appropriate categories. Encourage kids to be creative when filling in their slips of paper. "Doctor" is a profession but so are "pirate" and "ninja." Numbers can be small, large, or fractions. And a place can be ... anyplace.

Once you've collected slips of paper in the envelopes, say: **Some kids like to think about what they might do when they're grown-ups. They even have a plan—or at least the start of one.**

We'll take turns filling in this sentence: When I'm a grown-up I think I'll move to _____ (place) **where I'll work as a** _____ (profession), **have** _____ (number) **kids, and play with my pet** _____ (animal).

As for me, when I was younger I'd have completed that sentence this way ...

Share how you'd have filled in the blanks. Then pull one slip of paper from each envelope and fill in the sentence with the words you've drawn. It won't even be close to what you said first.

Have each child share his or her prediction for life and then pull out slips of paper and read aloud what the slips say. Expect hilarity to ensue.

After everyone has shared, say: **Life is full of surprises. We'll talk about surprises today. But before we dive into a surprise that came the way of a man named Peter, let's play a game of Whoozit!**

Amazing Animals Game

WHOOZIT
Time: about 10 minutes
Supplies: none

Ask kids to sit on the floor, and with books, chairs, or other objects, mark the area in which they'll play a game of tag that involves kids moving by scooting on their bottoms.

Explain that, when tagged, kids will freeze—no moving from that spot. What makes this game of tag unique is that you'll call out who's "It," and the It person will immediately change when you call out another name. When the It person changes, everyone frozen is instantly unfrozen and back in the game.

Vary how often you change who's It. Whether it's every 30 seconds, 10 seconds ... keep kids on their toes while they're scooting on their bottoms. And occasionally call out a category rather than a name. For example, "If you have a pet cat, you're now It!" or "If your birthday is in May, you're It" will launch a surprising variety of Its.

When you've finished playing, join kids in discussing:

- **What was most surprising about this game?**
- **What do you like about surprises—and what don't you like about them?**

When asking the following question, answer it first yourself, providing an age-appropriate example to model the sort of answer you're hoping to have shared by kids.

- **Tell about a time you weren't happy about a surprise. What was the surprise, and how did it all turn out?**

Amazing Animals Bible Story

A CAMPFIRE SURPRISE

Time: about 20 minutes
Supplies: Bible, paper, 5 or 6 sticks

Ask for a volunteer to serve as your sound effects person. Give that child two sheets of paper. Ask for a second volunteer to play the role of Peter.

Arrange the sticks on the floor as if you're building a campfire, and have everyone but Peter sit around the not-lit fire. Ask Peter to hover outside the circle.

Say: **Peter thought his loyalty to Jesus was unshakable. No way would he ever turn his back on Jesus—no matter what. Jesus knew better.**

Read aloud Luke 22:33–34.

Ask your sound effects person to crumple the sheets of paper and rub them together to make the sound of a fire burning.

Say: **When Jesus was arrested, Peter tried to defend Jesus—but Jesus was taken away. Here's what happened later that night …**

Slowly and with feeling, read aloud Luke 22:54–62. When the rooster crows, ask your sound effects person to make that sound.

When you've finished reading, join kids in discussing:

- **If you were Peter in this account, what would you be feeling and why?**
- **If you were the servant girl, what would you be feeling and why?**
- **If you were Jesus, what would you be feeling and why?**

Say: **Peter was surprised that he wasn't strong enough to stand up for Jesus. He was sad too, and maybe embarrassed. The rough, tough fisherman broke down in tears and ran away.**

But Jesus wasn't surprised. He knew what Peter could and couldn't do. He knew that Peter's fear would overcome him—three times.

And later, Peter was surprised again.

Read aloud John 20:19–21.

When Jesus greeted Peter and the other disciples, Jesus didn't yell at them for running away. Instead, Jesus greeted Peter and the others with words of peace.

Maybe it's no surprise that Jesus treats us the same way. He's not surprised when we don't live perfectly, when we sin. He knows we're not perfect and that's why we need him and his forgiveness.

And when we come to him asking for his help and forgiveness, he greets us the same way he greeted Peter: with words of peace and healing.

CLOSING PRAYER

NO-SURPRISE PRAYER

Time: about 5 minutes
Supplies: none

Ask kids to find a place in the room where they can be a bit apart from one another, and then to sit comfortably on the floor. Then ask them to lie on their backs and close their eyes.

Say: **You are now completely easy to hurt. I could surprise you by dropping a bowling ball on your tummy, and you wouldn't see it coming or be able to keep it from crushing you.**

I won't do that, by the way.

I will do this: I'll ask you to join me in silently thanking God for all the good surprises he sends our way.

God, thank you that there are no bowling balls falling. Or pianos. Or giant hail. Thank you that you protect us in ways we'd be surprised to see.

Please thank God for walking with you every day. (pause)

God, thank you for your surprisingly huge love for us. (pause)

God, thank you for surprising us with moments of joy and happiness. (pause)

God, thank you for the surprising friends who come our way. (pause)

And thank you, God, for forgiving us when we ask for it. And you forgive us not just once or twice, but a surprising, shocking, amazingly generous number of times. (pause)

Amen.

EXTRA-TIME ACTIVITY–OPTION 1

ROOSTER REMINDER

Time: about 10 minutes
Supplies: none

Say: **When a rooster crowed three times, Peter remembered what Jesus had told him earlier. That rooster was a reminder.**

We could use reminders of what Jesus tells us too.

Take the next two minutes to wander around the room and find one or two things that can remind you of something Jesus said or did. For instance, when I look at a clock, I can be reminded that Jesus said to always love God and others. That's something I can do all the time.

Let kids look around, and then have them report back. Affirm all the connections they've made.

Say: **The cool thing about having reminders about Jesus built into your life is that you never know when they'll show up. If I walk into my doctor's office and see a clock, I'll be reminded: Jesus asks me to love other people all the time. So I might look around the waiting room. Hmm ... I can pray for someone who looks sick, or I can start a conversation with a person who seems afraid.**

Let's thank God for those reminders we've found!

Lead kids in thanking God for the connections they've made, and invite God to surprise you all as you make those connections again and again in the weeks to come.

EXTRA-TIME ACTIVITY–OPTION 2

NO-TICKLE ZONE

Time: about 10 minutes
Supplies: none

Say: **Here's what we're not going to do—we're not going to grab the person next to us and tickle that person. Why? Because some of us are super ticklish and hate having others drive us crazy in that way.**

So let's do this: let's tickle ourselves.

Really.

Ask kids to try tickling the palms of their hands. When nobody's laughing, tell them maybe they should try tickling their ribs.

Say: **Still nothing? That's because there's no surprise in it. Your brain knows what's coming and cancels out the sensation.**

Ask kids to each find a partner and sit facing that person. Whoever is wearing the most colorful socks will be the first tickler. Be clear: Kids are tickling *only* the palms of their partner's right hand. *Nothing* else.

Have kids take turns tickling the palms of their partner's right hand. The sensation will be far more ticklish than when kids tried to tickle themselves.

Ask kids to discuss:

- **How did tickling yourself compare with being tickled? Which did you prefer?**
- **Tell about a time God surprised you in some way. What happened?**

EXTRA-TIME ACTIVITY–OPTION 3

SURPRISE ROOSTER ROUNDUP

Time: about 5 minutes

Supplies: none

Form kids into a circle and ask for one child to volunteer to be in the middle of the circle.

Explain that you'll spin the volunteer in circles as the volunteer keeps his or her eyes tightly closed. Then you'll point at someone in the circle who'll crow like a rooster. The volunteer will attempt to identify the rooster impersonator by the call only.

Have a large group of kids who don't know each other's names? Pause before starting and ask kids to share their names and one fun detail about themselves. That way your sightless volunteer can call out a name or a memorable detail.

How God Used
a Snake

The Point: God is powerful.
Scripture Connect: Acts 28:1–10

Supplies for all session 12 activities and options: masking (or painter's) tape, straws, cotton balls, balloons, stopwatch, paper, pens, Bible, lamp, empty 2-liter soda bottles without caps

The Basics for Leaders

There's power … and there's *unlimited power.*

Power is flipping a switch and flooding a room with light. It's punching a number into a phone and connecting with someone a continent away. It's climbing into a plane and soaring across an ocean in a matter of hours.

Unlimited power is scattering a million flaming suns through space to light a universe. It's connecting with everyone, in all time, all at once. It's waving a hand and creating oceans, dry land, the earth and all that's in it from … nothing.

Today you'll help your kids see how God has not just power, but unlimited power. And you'll help them discover how God uses his awesome, unlimited power to make himself and his purposes known.

OPENING ACTIVITY–OPTION 1

TELL ME THUMBTHING
Time: about 5 minutes, depending on attendance
Supplies: none

After kids arrive, say: **When people like a movie, they sometimes give it a thumbs-up.** Demonstrate. **Really like the movie? Two thumbs-up. If they dislike or really dislike the movie, they give it one or two thumbs-down.** Demonstrate.

Please rate how this past week has gone for you. Was it a one or two thumbs-up week? A one or two thumbs-down week? Or maybe you'd give it one thumbs-up and one thumbs-down—it was a good *and* bad week.

Rate your week now.

After kids rate their weeks, give kids 30 seconds each to explain why they rated their weeks as they did. You'll go first, sharing a story that models the sort of brief, personal stories you hope kids will share too.

Children will express themselves more over time, and hearing their stories will help you adapt this session to make it even more relevant to your kids' lives.

OPENING ACTIVITY–OPTION 2

HUFF & PUFF RELAY RACE

Time: about 5 minutes
Supplies: masking (or painter's) tape, straws, cotton balls

Create both start and finish lines by placing tape strips on the floor, about 10 feet apart. Then form kids into pairs and give each child a straw.

Explain: Pairs will separate—one partner will be behind the start line and one behind the finish line. Start-line partners will use their straws to blow a cotton ball across the finish line, but that's not the end of the race.

Finish-line partners will then use straws to blow their pair's cotton ball back across the start line.

Hand each start-line child a cotton ball. Tell kids that once cotton balls are placed on the floor behind the start line, there's no touching the cotton balls. The balls can *only* be moved by lung power.

Ask kids to assume their positions behind their cotton balls, and then clap once loudly to start the race. Once pairs have all completed the race, slap your forehead and announce: **Oh no! Now your cotton balls are all at the start line! Quick—blow them back behind the finish line to finish this race!**

After completing this unexpected final leg of the race, join kids in discussing:

- **As you moved your cotton ball along, did you feel awe-somely powerful? Why or why not?**

Say: **Moving a cotton ball across the floor isn't quite like pushing a giant boulder up a hill, but it did take some power. And so will playing a game of Slither Soccer!**

Amazing Animals Game

SLITHER SOCCER

Time: about 10 minutes
Supplies: balloons, masking (or painter's) tape, stopwatch

Form kids into two teams, the Rattlers and the Pythons. Place two 18-inch tape lines on the floor at opposite ends of the room to serve as goals.

Explain: Kids will play a game of soccer but will play the way snakes play—using only their heads to move the ball, because they don't have feet. Plus, they slither rather than run. And the entire game lasts just five minutes—with no time-outs.

After everyone lies down on the floor, toss an inflated balloon onto the field and let the snakes go at it. About two minutes into the game, toss a second balloon onto the field and then, with one minute left to play, a third balloon.

After the match ends ask both teams to give a mighty hiss (it's not like they can applaud!) and then sit together to discuss:

• **How do you feel? Was playing Slither Soccer tough or easy?**

Say: **If you were a snake, you'd hate playing soccer—it doesn't use any of your natural strengths.**

Snakes have to control their temperature by sunning themselves or finding shade, so soccer matches in the winter are out. Ditto for very hot days.

Snakes are usually solitary animals, so team sports don't work well for them.

And they shed their skin, which will make for a very messy field.

Sometimes we have to do things we're not good at either. Maybe we're great at math but have to write a story about Brazil. Or we're good at soccer but have to swim laps in a pool.

Good news! God is powerful, and when we're not strong he can work through and in us. A Jesus follower named Paul discovered that when he met an especially nasty snake.

Let's hear about how that happened!

Amazing Animals Bible Story

SNAKEBIT

Time: about 20 minutes
Supplies: paper, pens, Bible

Form kids into groups of three and give each group several sheets of paper and a pen.

Explain: **I'll read an account from the Bible about Paul, a shipwreck, and an annoyed snake. Each group will write a verse about something that happened in the account I read—a verse that can be sung to the tune of "Jesus Loves Me."**

Pause and lead kids in singing the first verse and chorus of "Jesus Loves Me" several times so it's fresh in their memories.

Then read aloud Acts 28:1–10.

When you've finished reading, ask kids to discuss:

- **In what ways did God show his power in this story?**
- **If you were one of the people living on Malta, would you want Paul to come back? Why or why not?**

Thank kids for sharing their thoughts; then ask them to get in their groups and write some verses.

Say: **You can write what you want, but one verse might be like the one I'll sing to you now …**

> **Paul got bit but didn't die.**
> **Everybody wondered why.**
> **Paul talked a lot about the Lord.**
> **With snakes around no one got bored.**

Give groups time to try to write a verse—five minutes will do it—and then it's time for them to sing their verses. Ask kids to sing what they've written, even if their verses aren't complete. A half-finished verse might inspire someone else to finish it!

When kids are done, applaud their efforts.

Then ask kids to discuss:

- When's a time you've seen God's power at work? Or have you not seen that?
- The Bible is full of powerful things Jesus did—raising the dead, turning water into wine, feeding thousands of people with a few fish and loaves of bread. If you could see with your own eyes one of Jesus's miracles, which would you pick—and why?

Say: **God is as powerful now as he was when he created the world. He's still doing awesome things in and through those who love him.**

Let's take a few minutes to praise our powerful God.

CLOSING PRAYER

LAMP PRAYER

Time: about 5 minutes
Supplies: lamp

Gather kids around the lamp. As much as possible, dim all other light in the room. Ask kids to face the lamp, and switch it on.

Say: **Let's thank God for shining his powerful light into our lives. Light that shows us who he is. That shows us who we are. That helps lead us to him.**

Ask kids to continue looking at the lamp as they offer aloud short prayers of thanks to God for what God has done—and is doing—for them.

Then ask kids to turn around and face away from the lamp.

Say: **Let's thank God for shining his powerful light through us into the lives of others. He uses us to bless others. To serve others. To help others.**

Ask kids to continue looking away from the lamp as they offer aloud short prayers of thanks to God for the privilege of serving him as we love and serve others.

When kids have finished, ask them to again turn toward the lamp and join hands with you and one another.

Pray: **God, you are powerful. You are the most powerful force ever—your creation proves it. Your love for us proves it.**

We praise you!

Amen.

EXTRA-TIME ACTIVITY-OPTION 1

THERE SHE BLOWS ... NOT

Time: about 10 minutes
Supplies: balloons (1 per child), empty 2-liter soda bottles without caps

This activity works as an illustration, but it's far more impactful if every child is able to actually try it. So ask neighbors to raid their recycling for empty bottles with narrow necks that you can stretch a balloon stem across.

Give each child a balloon and, if at all possible, a bottle.

Ask kids if they can blow up their balloon in a bottle. Most will say they can, but they're wrong.

Help kids lower their balloons into their bottles and then stretch the mouth of the balloon over the mouth of the bottle, sealing the bottle. Then ask kids to inflate their balloons.

They won't be able to do it.

The mass of the air in the bottles makes it impossible for the balloons to inflate. Kids can huff until their ears pop and their eyes bug out, but they'll still fail.

Gather kids in a circle and together discuss:

- **What's something you wanted to do but, even though you tried, you just weren't powerful enough to pull it off?**
- **What's something you could use our powerful God's help with this week?**

When kids have finished, thank them for sharing their thoughts and concerns.

EXTRA-TIME ACTIVITY-OPTION 2

ARM REST

Time: about 5 minutes
Supplies: stopwatch

Ask kids to stand apart and then lift their arms to shoulder height. Have kids hold that position—arms outstretched—for two full minutes as you tell about some age-appropriate challenge you're facing in life.

Encourage kids to keep their arms fully outstretched as you talk.

Say: **Thanks for listening. That's hugely helpful, but I'll bet your arms are tired. With your arms outstretched, form a circle and rest your arms on the shoulders of the people next to you.**

After kids are comfortably circled up, say: **Sometimes God shares his powerful encouragement and love through other people in our lives, like he did when you listened to me. Or like now when your friends are supporting you.**

Give someone a hug!

EXTRA-TIME ACTIVITY—OPTION 3

I'M SO STRONG I CAN ...

Time: about 5 minutes
Supplies: none

Gather kids in a circle.

Explain that they now all have super strength—they're so powerful they qualify for their own superhero movie and bobblehead doll.

Starting with you, you'll take turns silently acting out lifting something incredibly heavy or some other thing that only a superhero could do. For instance, maybe it's lifting a car or bending a steel rod with your bare hands.

Whatever it is, you'll act it out and the kids will guess what you're doing. When someone guesses correctly, it's time for the next person in the circle to silently act out a superhuman feat.

Keep guessing all around the circle.

Finish by saying: **What's amazing is that God can do all that—and far more!**

How God Uses
All Creatures
to Praise Him!

The Point: All God's creatures praise him.
Scripture Connect: Revelation 4:11; 5:11–13

Supplies for all session 13 activities and options: stopwatch; Bible; 2 balloons; leaves, stones, sticks, shells, or other objects from nature

The Basics for Leaders

We humans seem to think we've cornered the market on praising God. After all, we're the ones who've built churches, printed the Bible, displayed pictures of Jesus on the wall.

But we couldn't be more mistaken.

The truth is that *all* creation rings out with praise for God. *All* creatures reflect his creativity and power. And whether they know it or not, *all* his creatures ultimately rely on him for life.

In this session you'll help your kids discover that all God's creation—including your kids themselves—point back to him.

Whether aardvark, otter, or auk, all God's creation praises him.

And today your kids will pause to do just that.

OPENING ACTIVITY-OPTION 1

TELL ME THUMBTHING

Time: about 5 minutes, depending on attendance
Supplies: none

After kids arrive, say: **When people like a movie, they sometimes give it a thumbs-up.** Demonstrate. **Really like the movie? Two thumbs-up. If they dislike or really dislike the movie, they give it one or two thumbs-down.** Demonstrate.

Please rate how this past week has gone for you. Was it a one or two thumbs-up week? A one or two thumbs-down week? Or maybe you'd give it one thumbs-up and one thumbs-down—it was a good *and* bad week.

Rate your week now.

After kids rate their weeks, give kids 30 seconds each to explain why they rated their weeks as they did. You'll go first, sharing a story that models the sort of brief, personal stories you hope kids will share too.

Children will express themselves more over time, and hearing their stories will help you adapt this session to make it even more relevant to your kids' lives.

OPENING ACTIVITY-OPTION 2

NO-ME, NO-MY FUN ROUNDUP

Time: about 10 minutes
Supplies: stopwatch

Form kids into pairs and give them this assignment: they'll each tell their partner about something fun they did during the past week.

Except at no time can kids use the words *I, me,* or *my*. If someone uses one of those words, his or her partner will immediately interrupt by gobbling like a turkey.

Loudly.

Ask whichever partner is wearing the darkest socks to go first as the talker in each pair.

Say: **You'll talk for a solid two minutes about fun stuff you've done lately—and all without mentioning the three forbidden words: *I, me,* and *my*. If you forget and your partner gobbles, wait that out and then keep talking.**

Start ... now!

After two minutes, have partners switch who's talking and who's listening. Then when everyone's had the chance to talk, as a group discuss:

- **Was talking for two minutes without using those words easier or harder than you expected? Why?**
- **Tell about a time someone talked about him- or herself longer than you wanted to listen. Don't mention any names, please.**
- **Why do you think so many of us like talking about ourselves so much?**

Thank kids for sharing their thoughts, and then say: **It's fun talking about ourselves and what's happened to us. But here's a truth: things aren't always about us.**

Things are always about God though—because God is the Creator and he's always working in and through us. That's something we can praise him for.

Praising God means we notice him. We see what he's doing and who he is. We see how he's in our lives. And we share with him our thanks as we honor him in our hearts and with our actions.

We'll explore that a bit after we jump, crawl, and slither through an Animal Relay Race!

Amazing Animals Game

ANIMAL RELAY RACE
Time: about 10 minutes
Supplies: none

Form kids into two teams. Ask teams to huddle up, and have each choose a team name in 60 seconds or less.

After about a minute ask teams to, one at a time, shout out their team names.

Say: **Great names! Use those as you cheer your teammates on in our Animal Relay Race!**

Have teams line up against one wall, and explain that they'll be running a relay race to the far wall and back. The next person in line can't begin running until the teammate before them touches the wall.

And they won't be *running* the race exactly. Instead, they'll race the way a variety of animals might, were those animals hurrying to the far wall and back. You'll call out "Stop!" at different times and then call out an animal and how it moves. When you yell "Go!," the racers will continue the race … but moving like the animal you mentioned.

Vary how often you switch up the animals you call out to keep the race interesting and unpredictable. Here are animals and movements you can call out:

- Gallop like a horse
- Creep like a snail
- Slither like a snake
- Hop like a kangaroo
- Leap like a frog
- Scurry like an ant
- Slow-motion creep like a sloth

Once both teams have completed the relay, ask them to sit. Join them in discussing:

- You just impersonated lots of animals, from ants to kangaroos. Which animal that raced is your favorite? What is it about that animal that you like?
- If all creation is supposed to praise God—and that's what the Bible says—in what ways does the animal you just mentioned do that?
- You're part of creation too. In what ways do you praise God?

Amazing Animals Bible Story

SNEAK PEEK

Time: about 15 minutes
Supplies: Bible

Say: **God gave the apostle John a sneak peek at heaven. In the Bible book of Revelation, John wrote down a lot of what he saw and heard, and we're going to hear a bit of it now. Actually, you'll hear it as I read it to you.**

Ask kids to sit comfortably, close their eyes, and use their imaginations. Explain that you'll read a brief passage aloud and you want kids to imagine what John saw as they hear how he described the action.

Read slowly, pausing when appropriate to give kids time to "see" what John describes. And read with emotion—what's described is awe-inspiring.

Read aloud Revelation 5:11–13.

Pause a few seconds before inviting kids to open their eyes.

Say: **Turn to someone next to you and tell them how you pictured heaven. What did you see in your imagination as you listened to me read?**

Allow time for partners to talk, and then say: **I think it's incredible to imagine every creature in heaven and on earth and under the earth and in the sea singing praises to God.**

I have no idea how that would work, but I want to see it someday!

Ask kids to join you in discussing:

- **Picture yourself being a worm that lives under the earth. What would you have to praise God for?**
- **How about a child living in a poor country where there's a war? Or a child who's a refugee? What would that child have to praise God for?**
- **Do you think God's happier to hear us sing his praises or to see us praising him with our actions? Why do you answer as you do?**

After kids have finished talking, or you decide it's time to move on, say: **Let's take a few minutes to praise God right now!**

CLOSING PRAYER

BALLOON BOP PRAYER

Time: about 5 minutes
Supplies: 2 balloons

Inflate the balloons. Gather kids in the center of the room.

Say: **One way to praise God is to just recognize what he's done and who he is. For instance, I can praise God by saying *creation* because** that's something he did: God created the universe. I can praise him by saying *loving* because that describes who he is.

Explain that you'll praise God by keeping a balloon in the air. Every time someone bops it upward, that person is to call out a word or two that praises God.

Ask kids to pause and think of a few things God has done, or words that describe God. They can keep those words ready for when they bop the balloon.

Then toss a balloon up over the crowd of kids, and let the Balloon Bop Prayer begin! Feel free to add another balloon to keep the prayer really popping!

When the praises slow down, wrap up by praying: **God, thank you for being who you are—and for doing what you do. We praise you!**
Amen!

EXTRA-TIME ACTIVITY—OPTION 1

IN-YOUR-HAND NATURE

Time: about 10 minutes
Supplies: leaves, stones, sticks, shells, or other objects from nature; Bible

Before kids arrive, collect at least one small nature object for each child. Place them where kids will be able to access them easily.

Ask kids to each select one object. Encourage them to look closely at the objects they're holding as you read Romans 1:20 aloud.

Form kids into pairs and ask children to talk with their partners about this:

- **How do the objects you have show the power of God?**
- **How do the objects say that God is ... God?**

After kids have a chance to talk, ask pairs to show their objects and explain how they answered the questions.

Thank kids for participating, and then say: **God has left his fingerprints all over his creations ... including us. All God's creatures praise him!**

EXTRA-TIME ACTIVITY–OPTION 2

PRAISE POSTURE

Time: about 5 minutes
Supplies: stopwatch

Say: **Some people praise God by how they hold their bodies. Some kneel to show that Jesus is their King. Others bow their heads in respect. And some raise their hands to show praise.**

Ask kids to line up next to a wall, lean one shoulder against it, and then try as hard as they can to raise the arm pressed against the wall. They'll fail to raise their arms because they're leaning against the wall.

Ask kids to keep up the intense effort for two full minutes and to then step away from the wall. The arms that were leaning against the wall will rise automatically.

Say: **When you know God, it's almost impossible not to worship him somehow. Your praise almost flows out of you on its own.**

Now use that tired arm to give someone a high five!

EXTRA-TIME ACTIVITY–OPTION 3

ANIMAL ORCHESTRA

Time: about 10 minutes
Supplies: none

Gather kids in a semicircle and stand in front of them. Tell them they're now the official Animal Orchestra, and assign these parts: dogs, cats, cows, crows, chickens, and ask one child to be a rooster.

Quickly help kids practice their sounds aloud by making the animal sound and then having the appropriate kids repeat after you. If you have very few kids, it's okay to double up roles. If you have more than one child in a group, have that group stand slightly apart from the other groups of kids; each member of the Animal Orchestra needs to know when to make their sound.

What are the sounds? They're:

- Dogs: Woof!
- Cats: Meow!
- Cows: Moo!
- Crows: Caw!
- Chickens: Cluck!
- Rooster: Cock-a-doodle-doo!

Applaud kids' practice efforts and inform them that you're the orchestra conductor. You'll point to different groupings of kids, and when you do, those kids will make their animal sounds.

Announce that you'll lead the orchestra in playing "Jesus Loves Me." Point to different groups as you conduct the song. Add additional songs if you'd like—keeping them simple—to give your orchestra more to play.

When you've finished, thank your orchestra members and, as a group, discuss:

- **How do you think what you just experienced is like or unlike what John describes as all creatures singing God's praises?**
- **If you were to sing God's praises right now, what's a song you'd pick?**

If you have musical talent, or a child does, lead your group in singing a well-known praise song or two. If at all possible, sing together several of the songs mentioned by your kids.

Say: **God uses all his creatures to bring him praise!**